Another Time, Another Place

Raleigh Pitzer

This book includes several actual transcripts of past-life hypnotic regressions. All speech is quoted with dialects, accents, pronunciations, and language usage taken verbatim from each subject's recorded session with the author.

Cover design by Crystal Yaeger / **www.secretagent.com**

ISBN 1-58597-367-X

Library of Congress Control Number: 2005935336

4500 College Boulevard
Overland Park, KS 66211
888/888-7696
www.leatherspublishing.com

Dedicated to the memory of my son,
Frank Jeffry Pitzer.

Acknowledgments

Special thanks to my family for helping me with thousands of hours of research over the years.

And to all the people who have allowed me to use their transcripts, for without their trust this book could not have been written.

Also to Carl and Kay for teaching me the basic technique of hypnosis and opening my eyes and mind to what exists beyond the physical world.

Finally, none of this would have been possible if God had not allowed me access to this information.

Have you ever been somewhere new, yet it feels like you have been there before?

Do you have an unexplained fear of water, high places, or fire? Do you have a phobia as strange as the fear of eating cherry pie?

If so, the reason may be the result of something not in *your* lifetime but in the lifetime of someone else.

After more than 30 years and three continents of travel and research, I hope to offer you some answers you can apply to your own life.

CONTENTS

INTRODUCTION

◆ A Trellis with a Gate ◆

THE YEAR WAS 1969 and I had just graduated from high school. I decided to continue my education and chose aircraft mechanics as a career. I did not know then that moving to Kansas City would be a turning point in my life. That year I began a never-ending quest that has forever changed my life, as well as the lives of those who have known and seen me. I have been given the privilege of knowing what it is like on the other side after we die.

I had rented a small apartment in an older complex in the downtown area of K.C. It wasn't much, but I didn't mind it. Trying to work, go to school, and date seemed to be a full-time endeavor. I couldn't afford a telephone in my room, so all my calls were made from the pay phone in the hall. Luckily, the cord was long enough that I could lie down on the floor with my back to the wall, while I talked to my latest sweetie.

A broad spectrum of characters lived there. One carved tombstones for a living. Another was a store owner who had about 300 Nero jackets on hand when they went out of style (I wish I had a couple of them). Of course, there was also the caretaker of the grounds and his wife. Who could forget them? Their sexual exploits could be heard all over the entire building from the basement to where I lived on the third floor.

With all of this insanity going on, it certainly opened the eyes of a very naive young lad fresh off an Iowa farm. It didn't seem to bother me; in fact, it was kind of fun watching all these different events unfold. I learned a great deal about life in that short amount of time. I learned that it takes all types to make the world go around. Without these people, life would be very dull indeed.

As I was saying, I spent much of my spare time lying in the hall talking on the phone and watching all of this take place. Each evening an elderly couple who lived down another hall from me would pass by. They would always say, "Don't get up. It's okay, we'll just step over you." This got to be a regular ritual, and we would all get a laugh out of it. You know how sometimes when you meet someone you just naturally hit it off? That's how it was with this couple.

I didn't know their names and they didn't know mine, but they started calling me their son and we'd all laugh. One evening they asked me if I could join them for supper. They said I looked like I could use a good home-cooked meal, that I looked a little peaked. I told them sure (although I didn't think my cooking was that bad).

That evening we finally introduced ourselves. Her name was Kay and his was Carl. When we shook hands, I thought, "What huge hands this man has!" Carl said he was a professional magician and hypnotist. He must have seen the doubt in my eyes because he put on a magic show before we ate supper. Needless to say, I was impressed. Now that he had really gotten my attention, it was time to eat supper.

Kay was an excellent cook, and I have to admit there was a vast difference between our culinary styles. The meal was delicious, and I ate fried okra for the first time. It isn't my favorite food, but whenever I have some, I say, "Here's to you, Carl."

That evening we talked about our lives, and it was so comfortable that it seemed as though we had known each other forever. Carl and Kay had only been married for a few years, but because neither had children of their own, I seemed to fill that hole in their hearts. We spent a great deal of time together, and they got to know my personality pretty well.

One day I was worried about a test I was going to take, and it must have shown because they asked me what was wrong. When I told them my dilemma, Carl smiled slightly and asked if I trusted him. After I said yes, he told me to go get my books. Carl asked which pages I needed to know and then sat me down in a recliner and proceeded to hypnotize me. He had a small disc that had a spiral design on it. As he wiggled it, the spiral appeared to rotate. The next thing I remembered was waking up. My instructions were simple: don't look at the books at all and get a good night's sleep.

When I sat down the next day to take my test, my mind was a total blank! I panicked! I didn't know anything at all! After I finally accepted my fate and calmed down, I looked back down at my paper. This time, however, the answers appeared right before my eyes. Needless to say, I did very well.

Carl was almost as excited to ask me how I did on my test as I was to tell him. The next thing out of my mouth was, "I need to know more." I was privileged to be Carl's only student — with the promise to use my skills only for good. I still hold that agreement sacred.

One evening Carl said he felt it was time to show me something extraordinary that he had been working on for many years. He began by putting Kay to sleep — which was not unusual because she was always our guinea pig. Carl started regressing Kay down through her life very slowly. She was able to tell us about the smallest details in her life. You could tell that she was not just remembering, but actually experiencing, these events. For all practical purposes, she was there: hearing the conversations and smelling the smells. She had total recall of all her senses. Carl then took her to the very day she was born. Kay described all the things going on in the room at that time, including the people and their conversations. Kay was even able to tell us about seeing her mother for the very first time.

You could not have moved me from that chair with a pry bar! After all that, what else could there be? What I saw next has forever changed my life. Carl then regressed Kay to before she was born. There was a short pause, and then she began describing a trellis and a gate with beautiful flowers all around. That was as far as Carl could get Kay to go.

I was speechless! I wasn't sure what I had just seen, but something inside me said it was right. By the time Carl finally woke Kay up, her description had been so clear that you could picture it in your own mind.

I could hardly wait to try my own skills! With very little coaxing, my girlfriend was my first subject. Her mother died when she was born, but we overcame that obstacle and took that first step together to the other side. She became a Puritan girl who died when her cabin caught on fire. I wasn't certain what questions to ask, but I felt it went smoothly. In reality, my skills were very rough, but I learned enough to form the solid foundation I use today. I still have that set of small reel-to-reel tapes. Once in a while I even listen to them to remind myself of how far I've progressed.

Now, 30-plus years later, here are the actual transcripts of volunteers to my method. I tried to include a variety of stories. But before you read these transcripts, I should explain how this process is possible. Many people believe that the past life is the same as reincarnation. This is not the case! True reincarnation would only occur if an individual came back as himself, but that is not how God designed the system. Each of us has our own soul, and we all have a chance to get it right the first time around. Unfortunately, I have found that most of us still have things to learn and grow from after we pass on to the other side. Only the very innocent (usually children) retain their positions in heaven after death. It's almost as though we start out with all the knowledge we need, but lose it shortly after childhood. At that point, we have to start learning all over again. We make our own choices in life, but we are graded on those choices.

Unlike the law of physics in which no two items can share the same space at the same time, this is exactly what happens with a past life. It is as much a part of you as you are of it; however, you are still two separate entities. Jesus says in John 16:7, "Nevertheless I say to you the truth. It is to your advantage that I go away; for if I do not go away the Helper will not come to you; but if I depart, I will send Him to you." Jesus further explains this helper in John 14:16-17, 26. He says, "And I will pray the Father, and He will give you another Helper, that He may abide with you forever — the Spirit of Truth, whom the world cannot receive, because it neither sees Him nor knows Him; but you know Him, for He dwells with you and will be in you." Then in verse 26, Jesus says, "But the Helper, the Holy Spirit, whom the Father will send in My name, He will teach you all things, and bring to your remembrance all things that I said to you." The helper Jesus is telling us about is the past life I use hypnosis to talk to.

Now what I am about to say will certainly raise some eyebrows: the idea of past lives is not a new concept. Ancient Egyptian texts state the belief that the soul lives on after death and will return one day. In a more recent text, *The Bible*, we can read one of the most amazing stories on the subject. This amazing story is, in fact, the basis of Christianity; and without it, the religion today would be very different or possibly nonexistent. The story, found in the Book of John, is quite simple. There was a man named Jesus who was crucified and died on a cross. After his death, Jesus was then laid in a tomb with a stone placed across the door. What makes this story amazing is that eye witnesses said Jesus was able to rise from the dead, leave the tomb, and walk among the people once more. These facts are hard to argue with, and I am not going to since I believe them to be accurate.

According to Scripture, the first person to see the empty tomb was Mary Magdalene. Frantic in her quest to find her Lord, she came upon the gardener and asked him if he had seen the Lord because His body was gone. Mary did not realize the man she was speaking with was her Lord until He called her by name.

John 20: 11-16:

11 But Mary stood outside by the tomb weeping, and as she wept she stooped down and looked into the tomb.

12 And she saw two angels in white sitting, one at the head and the other at the feet, where the body of Jesus had lain.

13 Then they said to her, "Woman, why are you weeping?" She said to them, "Because they have taken away my Lord, and I do not know where they have laid Him."

14 Now when she had said this, she turned around and saw Jesus standing there, and did not know that it was Jesus.

15 Jesus said to her, "Woman, why are you weeping? Whom are you seeking?" She, supposing Him to be the gardener, said to Him, "Sir, if You have carried Him away, tell me where You have laid Him, and I will take Him away."

16 Jesus said to her, "Mary!" She turned and said to Him, "Rabboni!" (which is to say, Teacher).

Mary Magdalene was not Jesus' only friend who did not recognize Him by sight. Even His disciples mistook Him for a stranger, not once but several times. In both John 20: 19-20 and John 20: 24-28, it is written that Jesus had to show His disciples His wounds before they could recognize Him. Then in John 21: 1-14, Jesus proved to His disciples who He was by telling the men to cast their fishing net one last time. When they hauled it back up, their net was overflowing with 153 large fish — something Jesus had done when He was alive. They recognized Him by His actions not by His appearance.

These witnesses to Christ had either the world's shortest memories or they were actually seeing another's body with the soul of Christ walking and talking through it. Remember, these people had spent at least the last three years with Jesus, listening to His every word and watching His every movement. Loud speakers and PA systems didn't exist back then, and I doubt Jesus spent the final three years of His life shouting at everyone. No, I picture a quiet-spoken man, gentle of voice, yet heard and seen well by all in contact with Him. In the three days since His death, everyone either forgot what their Lord looked like or He no longer looked like Himself.

My grandfather has been gone for 30 years, but if I could see him today — that would be wonderful — I would easily recognize him. Granted, I might be a little shocked to see him, but then again, his final words were not that he would see me in 30 years. Jesus told His disciples He would rise in three days. Even though His body was gone, Jesus did rise again — but in a different body.

My intent is not to try to change anyone's religious beliefs, but to possibly strengthen them. I believe there is no such thing as one religion being better than the next. Who are we to say that a primitive tribe in a remote rain forest in South America may or may not have all the correct answers? As we face some of the most dangerous times in the history of mankind — most of which are due to religious disputes — it is time we become more tolerant of one another. What I bring to you is only one form of the same theme: there is a supreme being who watches over us, there is life after death, and there is more to life than the here and now.

EPISODE 1

◆ On a Hill ◆

FOR THIS FIRST episode, I would like to introduce a good friend of mine, John. Both he and his brother, Danny, have been working with me since about 1985. They are special to me because they were the first non-family members I ever used to assist on a missing-person case. The results were astounding, and they set the pattern which I still use today.

John is an aircraft worker with two children. He is talkative and friendly with his close friends, but others think he is a bit quiet and stays to himself. This episode is a wonderful example of how the past life and your present life are so closely intertwined. John was so impressed after his initial sessions that he and his wife named their first child Samantha (Sam for short).

Raleigh	*You are now going to another time, another place. What do you see?*
John	I'm not sure, I'm warm.
Raleigh	*You're warm, okay. Where are you at?*
John	On a hill.
Raleigh	*You're on a hill?*
John	Yes.
Raleigh	*Have you ever seen this hill before?*
John	I don't know.
Raleigh	*Do you live near the hill?*
John	I don't know. I'm watching a bird.
Raleigh	*You're watching a bird. How old are you?*

John	I can't make it out.
Raleigh	*What do you look like? Clear up the picture.*
John	I have a big nose.
Raleigh	*You have a big nose? What color of hair?*
John	I don't know. It's covered with fur.
Raleigh	*Covered with fur? Do you have a hat on?*
John	Sort of.
Raleigh	*A cap or something to cover your head?*
John	Yes, it's part of the coat.
Raleigh	*Part of the coat, okay. What is your name, or what are you called?*
John	I'm not sure.
Raleigh	*Okay.*
John	I see an image of a man in the trees looking at a bird.
Raleigh	*Okay. Where are you?*
John	I don't know.
Raleigh	*What country?*
John	I'm not sure. It's up on a hill with tall trees.
Raleigh	*Are they oak trees, pine trees, or what are they?*
John	Tall trees.
Raleigh	*Let's go to a time you happened to see someone else. Let's move away from the bird. What did you do after you got done watching the bird?*
John	I keep getting an image of a long beard.
Raleigh	*Whose beard?*
John	A man.
Raleigh	*Is it the man in the coat?*
John	Yes.
Raleigh	*Who is the man in the coat?*
John	Not sure, mid-30s, looks like he hasn't been cleaned for a while.

Raleigh	*Let's go to where the man is moving and doing something else. What do you see?*
John	He's by a river.
Raleigh	*What's he doing?*
John	Checking traps.
Raleigh	*Traps, okay. What is the year?*
John	Not sure.
Raleigh	*What do you think it is?*
John	Eighteen ....
Raleigh	*Eighteen what?*
John	1860.
Raleigh	*That's what you think it is?*
John	Everything looks untouched.
Raleigh	*Okay, let's go to a point where this man sees other people.*
John	I see.
Raleigh	*Who is he with?*
John	Not sure. [Acting uncomfortable.]
Raleigh	*Are you in pain?*
John	No, thirsty.
Raleigh	*Why are you thirsty?*
John	I haven't had a drink.
Raleigh	*Why not?*
John	I've been working in the hills.
Raleigh	*Okay, do you see people yet?*
John	Yes.
Raleigh	*Okay, who are they?*
John	I don't know. They live in a cabin.
Raleigh	*Is it a big cabin?*
John	No, little.
Raleigh	*Is it your cabin?*
John	No, they're giving me beef jerky. They're some salt out of the bay.

Raleigh	*Is it your bay?*
John	No.
Raleigh	*Did you tell them your name?*
John	I think I did.
Raleigh	*Let's go to where you did. What was your name?*
John	They kept calling me, "Stranger."
Raleigh	*Did you tell them your name?*
John	I don't think so. We didn't talk much, only what we needed.
Raleigh	*Are you a nice man or a mean man?*
John	Quiet.
Raleigh	*Where are you?*
John	In the cabin. There's a young girl dragging some wood out.
Raleigh	*What's she doing?*
John	She's pulling it out and putting it right in the stove.
Raleigh	*Are you saying anything to the girl?*
John	No.
Raleigh	*Is she saying anything to you?*
John	No, looks like she's been hit on quite a bit.
Raleigh	*Like beat?*
John	Yes.
Raleigh	*Who beat her?*
John	I guess the man who runs the store.
Raleigh	*What's the name of the store?*
John	No name, it's like a trading post.
Raleigh	*Where is this located? What part of the country?*
John	I don't know. It's in the clearings.
Raleigh	*What part of the country do you think you're in?*
John	It's cold at night.
Raleigh	*Are you in the United States?*
John	I think so because the girl is Indian.

Raleigh	*What do they call her?*
John	All they call her was "Bitch."
Raleigh	*What type of Indian is she?*
John	I don't know. I feel sorry for her, but it is none of my business. She didn't do nothin'.
Raleigh	*What type of Indian is she?*
John	Umm, Navajo.
Raleigh	*What makes you think that?*
John	Feathers and beads on her neck.
Raleigh	*They are Navajo beads?*
John	I think so. They are red, white, black, and a blue one in the center.
Raleigh	*Is there an emblem or anything?*
John	No, but I can't make it out.
Raleigh	*Where did you go after you left the store?*
John	I went back to check the traps.
Raleigh	*Did you catch anything?*
John	Some beaver for pelts.
Raleigh	*Let's come ahead a little more. Did you ever see any other people than those at the store?*
John	The Indians are making me nervous.
Raleigh	*Why?*
John	They are watching me.
Raleigh	*Do they bother you?*
John	No, but they are watching.
Raleigh	*What do they call you?*
John	I … I … don't know.
Raleigh	*But the Indians are watching. How do you know?*
John	I've seen a couple behind trees.
Raleigh	*What kind of Indian are they?*
John	I don't know for sure. They look hungry.
Raleigh	*They look hungry?*

John	Yes.
Raleigh	*Let's go to a time either forward or back where you knew what your name was.*
John	I don't know why, but I keep thinking it's Sam.
Raleigh	*Where do you think you originally came from?*
John	I see a young boy kicking a ball.
Raleigh	*Is the young boy you?*
John	It's all I see.
Raleigh	*Let's come to a time where you see people.*
John	There's a picket fence.
Raleigh	*What about the fence?*
John	It's inside of a town.
Raleigh	*What's the name of the town?*
John	I'm not sure, but it's nice.
Raleigh	*Let's come to a time where you saw your family, your parents, or whoever is taking care of you.*
John	My ma.
Raleigh	*What does your mom look like?*
John	She's pretty.
Raleigh	*She's pretty?*
John	Her hair, it's like a bee hive.
Raleigh	*It's like a bee hive, okay. What's she wearing?*
John	She just bought a dress.
Raleigh	*What is she doing at this moment?*
John	She's waving at a boy to come in.
Raleigh	*She's waving at a boy to come in?*
John	I think so.
Raleigh	*Is it a boy you know?*
John	I don't know. It's all I see.
Raleigh	*What is she saying?*
John	"Put the ball away, time to eat, and got to do chores."
Raleigh	*Does she say your name?*

John	Yes.
Raleigh	*What is it?*
John	Samuel.
Raleigh	*Samuel? Samuel what? I know you have heard it before. You may have also written it down. Correct?*
John	I don't remember.
Raleigh	*What's your mother's name?*
John	Elizabeth.
Raleigh	*You think it's Elizabeth. Okay, what is the year? Somewhere in your home something probably had the date on it. What is it?*
John	Not sure, she's yelling at me.
Raleigh	*What for?*
John	To clean my room.
Raleigh	*Did you do it?*
John	Yeah.
Raleigh	*Okay, she's not yelling at you now. Do you understand? This has already happened. Are you beginning to understand that?*
John	Yeah.
Raleigh	*So this has already happened. So, what is the year?*
John	I think it's '46.
Raleigh	*1846?*
John	Yeah.
Raleigh	*Okay, what is the name of the town?*
John	Not sure, I don't know much about reading.
Raleigh	*What have people said it was?*
John	I don't know. There's just a bunch of cowboys, and I'm not allowed in the saloon.
Raleigh	*Okay. What is your last name, Samuel?*
John	I think it's Bennett.

Raleigh	Bennett, okay, very good. Now we are returning a few years, to you as an adult. I want you to remember this has already happened. You will only be describing the sights that you see. You will not be reliving them, only describing them. Alright?
John	Yes.
Raleigh	Okay. How did Samuel Bennett die? Let's go to the day Samuel Bennett died. What happened that day? You are only describing, not feeling, what happened.
John	I got robbed.
Raleigh	You got robbed?
John	Yes.
Raleigh	Who robbed you?
John	Indians.
Raleigh	The Indians robbed you?
John	Yes, they took my hare.
Raleigh	Okay, where were you when they did this?
John	I was checking on my traps near the creek, and one came out of the water.
Raleigh	One came out of the water? He was hiding there?
John	Yes, he must have been. I'm not sure. It happened so fast.
Raleigh	How many were there?
John	There were three.
Raleigh	Were they the same ones that had been watching you?
John	Not sure. Couldn't tell the faces.
Raleigh	Okay, were you able to protect yourself at all?
John	My knife.
Raleigh	With your knife? Did you kill any of the Indians?
John	I don't think so.
Raleigh	How did they kill you?
John	They hit me on the back of the head.

Raleigh	*With what?*
John	A stone.
Raleigh	*A stone?*
John	A sharp stone.
Raleigh	*Was it just a stone, or was it a tomahawk?*
John	It did have a handle.
Raleigh	*You are close enough now. What type of Indians were they?*
John	I don't know. They wore three feathers on their head … with black tips. White feathers with black tips.
Raleigh	*What tribe did that represent?*
John	I … I don't know. They threw me in the water.
Raleigh	*Were you already dead when they threw you in the water?*
John	I don't think so. I was in pain.
Raleigh	*What are the Indians doing right now?*
John	Taking my boots and my pelts.
Raleigh	*Had you done anything to aggravate these Indians?*
John	I don't think so.
Raleigh	*Alright, why did you come to where you were, to live by yourself? Why did you come alone?*
John	Don't like people.
Raleigh	*Why don't you like people?*
John	They are mean to each other.
Raleigh	*Okay, how long have you been away from your family? Mother and father?*
John	Quite a while.
Raleigh	*Were they alive, or were they dead?*
John	They were gone.
Raleigh	*How did they die?*
John	My ma got sick.
Raleigh	*What happened to your dad?*

John	Never did know.
Raleigh	*Okay, have you died yet?*
John	Yes, I'm laying here alone in the water.
Raleigh	*Are the Indians gone?*
John	Yes.
Raleigh	*Did anyone ever find you after you died?*
John	I don't see. It's just me laying in the water.
Raleigh	*Were you ever found?*
John	No.
Raleigh	*What is happening after you die? Where do you go?*
John	I see a white mist.
Raleigh	*Okay, where is this white mist?*
John	Everything's dark around me.
Raleigh	*Did you go to heaven?*
John	I don't know. I know it's peaceful, feels good.
Raleigh	*Did you ever meet God?*
John	I don't see.
Raleigh	*Let's go to the first person you see. Describe the first person you meet after you died.*
John	A man.
Raleigh	*What about the man?*
John	Long wavy hair.
Raleigh	*Long wavy hair. Who is this man?*
John	It's so peaceful.
Raleigh	*Does he say anything to you?*
John	Just smiles.
Raleigh	*Okay, what does his face look like?*
John	Kind of long. Short beard, real short beard.
Raleigh	*Who is this man?*
John	I don't know.
Raleigh	*Have you seen him before?*
John	No.

Raleigh	*Okay, what is he doing right now other than just smiling?*
John	Just smiling.
Raleigh	*Are you any closer to him?*
John	No.
Raleigh	*What is the first thing that man says to you?*
John	Something peace, something peace with God.
Raleigh	*Okay, say exactly what was said and the way it was said. It's very clear to you now. It has already happened.*
John	"Join God in peace."
Raleigh	*Join God in peace?*
John	Yes.
Raleigh	*Was that all He said?*
John	I think so.
Raleigh	*Before we come back to John, why did you come back to John?*
John	I never had nobody.
Raleigh	*You never had nobody. Why did you come back to John?*
John	I wanted to have a son.
Raleigh	*Will John have a son?*
John	I think so.
Raleigh	*What makes you think that?*
John	His blood line.
Raleigh	*What about his blood line?*
John	All boys. [John is one of four brothers.]
Raleigh	*So you're sure he will have a son.*
John	Yes. [John's second child is a boy.]
Raleigh	*Is John happy?*
John	He's nervous.
Raleigh	*Are you helping?*
John	In a small way.

EPISODE 2

◆ Castle Gates ◆

I MET MIKE many years ago when my family and I moved to the Wichita area in 1975. He and his family lived in the same apartment building that we did. Since almost all of us in the complex had moved there from distant areas, we became one huge family. We got together at least once or twice a week, and soon everyone knew I was a hypnotist. Before long, everyone wanted to be regressed to a past life.

This story reminds us that although certain times in history have been romanticized, that was not necessarily the truth. Even in a time of chivalry, there was still great cruelty. Not all knights were knights in shining armor.

Raleigh	*We're going to go back now to a time and a place you know nothing about. This is before you were born. To another time, another place. What do you see?*
Mike	Castle gates.
Raleigh	*Castle gates. What about the castle?*
Mike	Lots and lots of people coming in. Lots of people coming in.
Raleigh	*Okay, what's the year?*
Mike	14 … 14 … 58.
Raleigh	*Is it 1458?*
Mike	July … July 12th, 1458.
Raleigh	*Okay, what's your name?*
Mike	They call me by my father's trade.

Raleigh	*And what is that?*
Mike	He sells fruit in the market.
Raleigh	*Okay, so what do they call you?*
Mike	Because of my hair, they call me Golden … Golden.
Raleigh	*Golden what?*
Mike	Just … just Golden.
Raleigh	*Just Golden? Okay, how old are you?*
Mike	I think I've seen 12 winters.
Raleigh	*Okay, you have seen 12 winters or you are 12 years old?*
Mike	My father has told me I have been through 12 long winters with him.
Raleigh	*Where are you? What country is this?*
Mike	Ours is a little town … St. Petersburg, in England.
Raleigh	*What do you look like?*
Mike	Kind of raggedy clothing, but kept clean.
Raleigh	*Okay, what's your mother's name?*
Mike	Father says Mother has been dead for three winters.
Raleigh	*Okay, but what was her name? And what was your father's name?*
Mike	Father.
Raleigh	*Did you ever hear your father's name?*
Mike	Yes, they call it at the market.
Raleigh	*What was it?*
Mike	I don't … I just can't say it.
Raleigh	*Alright, did your father raise all these vegetables?*
Mike	We had fruit trees.
Raleigh	*Fruit? You mean like apples and things?*
Mike	Right, apples … peaches ….
Raleigh	*Did you have any brothers or sisters?*
Mike	No, I was the only one.
Raleigh	*The only one, okay. Are you in the castle right now?*

Mike	We are waiting for them to open the gates to let us in.
Raleigh	*What is the name of the castle? Does the castle have a name?*
Mike	Yes, it's the castle of the Lord of Huntington.
Raleigh	*Who is the Lord of Huntington?*
Mike	Some people say the Lord of Huntington was Robin Hood. But nobody knows for sure.
Raleigh	*Was there such a person as Robin Hood?*
Mike	He'd been good to the people, they say.
Raleigh	*Did you ever know a true instance of Robin Hood?*
Mike	I never seen him myself, but I've heard many tales of his men. And my father says he is a great man.
Raleigh	*Okay, you say Robin Hood is the Lord of Huntington. Who owns the castle?*
Mike	The castle belongs to the Lord of Huntington.
Raleigh	*Okay, the day you go into that city, was that the day you died?*
Mike	No, riders came at us from behind.
Raleigh	*Where were you?*
Mike	We were on the road.
Raleigh	*Was your father with you?*
Mike	Yes.
Raleigh	*How old were you?*
Mike	Seventeen. They came from behind ....
Raleigh	*Okay. But now you are at the market. When was this? How old were you?*
Mike	Fifteen.
Raleigh	*Fifteen. You were 15, okay, very good. You never got married, then?*
Mike	No.
Raleigh	*Okay, did your father ever remarry?*

Mike   Father would never remarry.

Raleigh   *What was your father's last name?*

Mike   Joseph … Joseph ….

Raleigh   *Did you ever hear his last name?*

Mike   Joseph … Joseph …. Everybody called him Joe for short.

Raleigh   *Did you ever hear a last name?*

Mike   I don't remember.

Raleigh   *Okay, very good. Alright, let's come up now. When you got older, did anyone call you anything else?*

Mike   As I got older ….

Raleigh   *What did your girlfriend call you?*

Mike   She always used to tease me about my golden hair, too.

Raleigh   *What did she call you? What was your actual name?*

Mike   Gold … Golden was what my father named me.

Raleigh   *Oh! That was your actual name?*

Mike   Yes.

Raleigh   *Oh, so what'd your girlfriend call you?*

Mike   She used to call me Straw Hawk.

Raleigh   *Straw Hawk? Did that make you mad?*

Mike   Sometimes, because the straw fields where we used to have to sleep would be of a golden color. My father said that's how I got the color of my hair.

Raleigh   *Okay, let's come up to when you were 17 years old. You were on that road. Did your father die the same day?*

Mike   Yes. Father and I. Both.

Raleigh   *Okay, how did it happen? Remember, this has already happened, hasn't it?*

Mike   Yes.

Raleigh   *So you're just describing what happened.*

Mike	Father and I are walking down ... down the road .... Riders ... riders behind us.
Raleigh	*Who were the riders?*
Mike	Men from another castle.
Raleigh	*Were you at war?*
Mike	Times were hard and the people were fighting because of all the crime and the scandal of Robin Hood. Times were bad.
Raleigh	*Was there an actual person as Robin Hood? What was his real name?*
Mike	No one knew his real name, just Lord of Huntington.
Raleigh	*Did you ever see him?*
Mike	I saw the Lord of Huntington, yes.
Raleigh	*You did?*
Mike	Yes.
Raleigh	*What did he look like?*
Mike	He was tall ... reddish brown hair .... Well, well-dressed.
Raleigh	*Okay, can you picture him right now in your mind?*
Mike	Yes, we're at the market.
Raleigh	*Okay, was he friendly to you?*
Mike	Yes, very. Always.
Raleigh	*How many times did you see him?*
Mike	Many times more.
Raleigh	*How tall was he?*
Mike	About ... six foot ... he stood very tall.
Raleigh	*How did he dress?*
Mike	Very, very well-dressed for an Englishmen.
Raleigh	*Very well-dressed?*
Mike	Yes, they always were.
Raleigh	*What weapons did he use?*

Mike   He was carrying a sword on his right side.

Raleigh   *Did the people of the kingdom know who he was?*

Mike   Everybody said he was Robin Hood, but nobody would say who.

Raleigh   *Who was the king at the time?*

Mike   King Richard was still King at the time … but they were getting intolerant of him as King. It was getting like … for a long time … people were afraid at the time. Times were really bad.

Raleigh   *How old are you right now?*

Mike   Fifteen.

Raleigh   *Were you tall or short?*

Mike   Tall for my family.

Raleigh   *Okay, how tall were you?*

Mike   I stood to the shoulders of the man they called Robin Hood.

Raleigh   *What did Robin Hood say to you? Was he friendly?*

Mike   Always friendly.

Raleigh   *What things would he say?*

Mike   "Through all these things, it's nice to see happy people at the market."

Raleigh   *What things?*

Mike   We would be at war.

Raleigh   *War with who?*

Mike   France.

Raleigh   *Okay, who was coming from France? Who was the leader of France?*

Mike   Father never said …. He just … said the French were bad.

Raleigh   *Was your father wise?*

Mike   I thought he was.

Raleigh   *Was he?*

Mike	He used to drink all our money away. So we could never move from the village.
Raleigh	*Okay. Did you drink?*
Mike	No. I have dranken, but Father is ....
Raleigh	*What was your favorite drink?*
Mike	We used to go down to the village, and if we could get the maid to give us some ale from their mugs, we used to drink the ale.
Raleigh	*Did you have to pay for the ale?*
Mike	No, they would give it to us to get us drunk and then watch us stumble around.
Raleigh	*Did you like that?*
Mike	Ale was good; but what was better, when you get drunk, they give you the bread and cheese.
Raleigh	*What would you do with the bread and cheese?*
Mike	Keep half of it for later and eat half then.
Raleigh	*Did you feel bad about having to do that?*
Mike	Yes, but later I'd have something to eat when I was hungry.
Raleigh	*Okay, what would your diet consist of? What was your main food?*
Mike	We ate our foods that we made. And Father would sometimes have enough to buy game, birds, and pheasant. Every now and then he would buy something a little bigger.
Raleigh	*How much would a pheasant cost?*
Mike	A pheasant — a fairly good-sized one — would cost us tuppence.
Raleigh	*How much?*
Mike	Tuppence.
Raleigh	*A tuppence?*
Mike	Yes.

Raleigh	*Okay, did you ever buy like beef, meat?*
Mike	Not very often. Mostly fish, fish and bird.
Raleigh	*What would fish cost?*
Mike	You could buy four, five, six good fish for sometimes threepence. And you could buy eight, nine … eight or nine real, real good fish for sixpence.
Raleigh	*How much would a fish like that weigh? A good fish?*
Mike	A nice fish would weigh three, three-and-a-half pounds.
Raleigh	*Okay, what kind of fish would that be?*
Mike	Flounder.
Raleigh	*A flounder?*
Mike	Yes.
Raleigh	*Okay. What was your favorite food? If you had your favorite food, what would it be?*
Mike	When Father would have enough to buy a pig and we could have roast pig.
Raleigh	*Roast pig … that was your favorite?*
Mike	Yes.
Raleigh	*Alright, let's come up now to the time when your father and you were killed. How did it happen? The people were coming up behind you.*
Mike	Father … they stopped Father and said had we seen any … anybody on the road. Father said no, we hadn't. And the man reached down and slapped him once and said, "Liar!"
Raleigh	*Did you see someone?*
Mike	No, nobody. Nobody had rode … rode down that road.
Raleigh	*Okay, where were those people from?*
Mike	I hadn't seen them. Their colors were ….
Raleigh	*Were they knights?*

Mike	Yes … silver. Silver and copper armor, with blue and white mascot.
Raleigh	*Did they have a hood on?*
Mike	Yes, they were dressed in armor.
Raleigh	*Okay, how many of them were there?*
Mike	There was … there was a quarry of 14 of them, all together.
Raleigh	*Okay, were they all dressed in armor?*
Mike	Yes, all with blue and white mascot.
Raleigh	*Okay, they were all dressed the same?*
Mike	Yes.
Raleigh	*Okay, same colors and … everything?*
Mike	Yes, same all. They looked like they were going to a castle … castle for the games.
Raleigh	*What was their symbol? Did they have a symbol?*
Mike	They had a crest of a … of a falcon with one wing spread, one wing closed.
Raleigh	*That was it?*
Mike	Yes.
Raleigh	*Okay, then what happened?*
Mike	Father got angry and yelled back.
Raleigh	*Was he drunk?*
Mike	No, he hadn't … he hadn't been drinking this day. It was hot.
Raleigh	*Did he usually argue like that?*
Mike	No, but … but Father was an honest man, had never lied.
Raleigh	*Okay, he was mad about the lying.*
Mike	Yes.
Raleigh	*Alright ....*

Mike   The man got down from his horse, walked over to Father, pushed him on the ground. And then I went over and jumped!

Raleigh   *You jumped on the knight?*

Mike   Yes … he threw me down, too, and then ordered his men to search us. They dumped our wagon out … all our fruit. And they took Father's money. Father was screaming.

Raleigh   *What was he saying?*

Mike   "Don't take our money! It's all we have! It's all … it's all … it's all for the boy! Don't take the money! Please!" [Mike gets more and more upset as we proceed.]

Raleigh   *Okay, it all happened. Remember, you're just describing what happened. Remember?*

Mike   Yes.

Raleigh   *Okay, so then what did they say?*

Mike   Father pleaded. One of the other knights came up … and counted the money and said there was not enough money to pay for taxes on the fruit that we had. And said either to come up with the money or we would die! Father … Father was scared now. I could see the look in his face.

Raleigh   *How much money was there?*

Mike   We had … we had a little less than four crowns.

Raleigh   Okay, how much did they say you needed?

Mike   They said we needed four and six.

Raleigh   *Six what?*

Mike   Four crowns, six schillings.

Raleigh   *Okay, did you have the six schillings?*

Mike   No. We said they could take the fruit, but they didn't want that. They have Father now!

Raleigh	*Did they kill him then?*
Mike	One man's taking out a … taking out a dagger …. He … he stabs him ….
Raleigh	*Okay, remember this has all happened, didn't it?*
Mike	Yes.
Raleigh	*Okay, it's painful, I'm sure, but it already happened and it can't be changed. Right?*
Mike	Yes.
Raleigh	*Alright, now what happened? Did they kill him then, right then?*
Mike	Father's screaming, laying on the ground screaming. There's blood all over him. I'm trying to get to him, but they won't let me.
Raleigh	*Is that when they killed you?*
Mike	No! Father yelled, "Run! Run!" I broke loose and ran. I could hear them behind me, chasing me.
Raleigh	*Were they on their horses?*
Mike	Yes. Two were chasing me with lances … lances …. I couldn't outrun a horse. A horse! I could see them getting closer ….
Raleigh	*Okay, remember this has all happened, didn't it? Okay, did they kill you with the lance?*
Mike	I tripped and I'm … I'm laying there, and he's … standing above me laughing. He has his lance pointed right at me … right at me.
Raleigh	*Did he kill you then?*
Mike	It's … it's pointing at me!
Raleigh	*What did he say? Did he say anything?*
Mike	It's sharp! His laugh …. [Getting VERY upset.]
Raleigh	*REMEMBER … Remember, this has already happened! Right?*
Mike	Laughing! He's laughing!

Raleigh	*Okay, alright, remember this has already happened, didn't it?*
Mike	Yes.
Raleigh	*Okay, and you know you're just telling about it now, right?*
Mike	Yes.
Raleigh	*You know you have been dead for a long time. Isn't that true?*
Mike	Yes.
Raleigh	*Okay, so you know that couldn't be changed.*
Mike	Yes.
Raleigh	*Okay. Did he kill you with the lance then?*
Mike	He's poking it … slowly … and it hurts!
Raleigh	*He poked it in slowly?*
Mike	Yeah, and I can feel it pressing … but he's laughing … laughing ….
Raleigh	*Okay, okay ….*
Mike	I can feel it. It's hard to breathe. [Spoken as if with his final breath.]
Raleigh	*Okay, have you died?*
Mike	Yes.
Raleigh	*There's no pain anymore, is there?*
Mike	No.
Raleigh	*Now, can you see the people behind you?*
Mike	Nobody, they just rode off and left us.
Raleigh	*They just rode off and left you. Did your father die right away?*
Mike	Father … Father is dead.
Raleigh	*Was he dead before you?*
Mike	Yes.
Raleigh	*Okay, now I want you to describe what happened after you died. Okay? What happened after you died?*

Mike	Funny feeling … floating, just going back to all the places I had been. And running into people I knew. Nobody could see me, but I could see them. Father's … Father's friends would ask … would ask, "Where did Joseph go?" People would say he's on the road … on the road traveling and he would be back.
Raleigh	*Did they ever find out?*
Mike	Later that day, a rider from the village found us in the road and brought us back to town in a cart.
Raleigh	*Did anyone mourn you?*
Mike	All our friends came, and we were taken to the church.
Raleigh	*Was your father with you?*
Mike	Yes, we were both there.
Raleigh	*I mean, you were seeing yourself being taken to the church.*
Mike	They brought Father, too.
Raleigh	*Yes, but was your father's spirit with you?*
Mike	I don't know … I never ….
Raleigh	*Alright, you don't know if he was there or not.*
Mike	No, I felt all alone. I wished he would be.
Raleigh	*Did they ever find the men that killed you?*
Mike	No.
Raleigh	*Who did they turn out to be? Did you ever find out who they were?*
Mike	No.
Raleigh	*What year is it now?*
Mike	Lost track of years, but … but King Richard has gone into hiding. And they say that he will … he's going to meet with Robin Hood on the shore. And come back to England and take his rule again.

Raleigh	*What have you been doing all this time?*
Mike	Just floating … looking … I feel so empty.
Raleigh	*Looking at what?*
Mike	People I used to know and how they are growing up.
Raleigh	*Did you ever go other places? Like other countries?*
Mike	I floated, I felt … I felt for different places but always come back. Traveled … traveled all over.
Raleigh	*You traveled all over?*
Mike	Yes. Many different places.
Raleigh	*What were a few of the places you went to?*
Mike	Went to … went to France to see how the French acted, why they didn't like the English.
Raleigh	*Did you find out why?*
Mike	No, they just called us … called us fools to follow King Richard.
Raleigh	*Okay, where else did you go?*
Mike	To Spain …. Spain was beautiful.
Raleigh	*Where was your favorite place that you went to see?*
Mike	To a little town …. Father used to take me there when I was small … every summer …. This side of Norfolk.
Raleigh	*Did you ever go to heaven?*
Mike	Yes, I did. People were all friendly.
Raleigh	*Where did you go that you met these friendly people?*
Mike	Just all sort of light and wide, wide open. Buildings with no gates, no doors. Never cold. Just travel free from place to place.
Raleigh	*Did you talk to those people? Did the other people talk to you?*
Mike	I could see their mouth, but never hear any words.
Raleigh	*That was in that city?*

Mike Yes, it was beautiful!

Raleigh *Okay, what did it look like?*

Mike Solid bright! Bright! No … no … nobody fighting or hurting each other.

Raleigh *Okay, was that heaven?*

Mike It must have been!

Raleigh *Was it?*

Mike I remember dying …. I remember floating, floating up.

Raleigh *Where was this city located?*

Mike Above … above the people below us. We could look down and watch.

Raleigh *You could watch them below you?*

Mike Yes.

Raleigh *How far above everybody were you?*

Mike We were way up … but we could come down and see everything they were doing.

EPISODE 3

◆ A Shipping Dock ◆

I WOULD LIKE you to meet Kurt. He is a design engineer for a major aircraft company. Kurt is a family man, with a wife and two children.

I wanted to include this story because it shows how closely intertwined people are with their helpers. Nothing has happened in Kurt's life to cause a phobia of high places or water, but he is afraid of both. Although Kurt has learned how to swim, his life has still been influenced by his helper, Eric.

Raleigh	*We are now going to another time, another place. A place you know nothing of. What do you see?*
Kurt	I'm near the dock.
Raleigh	*What type of dock is it?*
Kurt	Where the ships come in.
Raleigh	*Are you alone?*
Kurt	No, someone is with me.
Raleigh	*Who is with you?*
Kurt	Albert.
Raleigh	*Who is Albert?*
Kurt	He is my best friend.
Raleigh	*Why are you at the dock?*
Kurt	We are looking to see what the ships have just brought in.
Raleigh	*What do you see?*

Kurt	Nothing really. They have only started to unload their cargo, so there is only a few boxes around and some horses.
Raleigh	*Where were you going?*
Kurt	To the mercantile.
Raleigh	Do you have money?
Kurt	No.
Raleigh	*How old are you?*
Kurt	Nine.
Raleigh	*Are you from a well-to-do family or a poor one?*
Kurt	A well-to-do.
Raleigh	*What is your name?*
Kurt	Eric.
Raleigh	*What are you doing right now?*
Kurt	Trying to catch a chicken.
Raleigh	*Ha-ha. A chicken? What color is it?*
Kurt	Red.
Raleigh	*Is it a rooster?*
Kurt	Yes.
Raleigh	*What is your idea of catching the chicken?*
Kurt	To have Albert chase it toward me and I'll put a sack over it.
Raleigh	*Did it work?*
Kurt	Yes, now we don't know what to do with it.
Raleigh	*Ha-ha, that was my next question. What did you do with it?*
Kurt	We just looked at each other and shrugged our shoulders and decided to let it go.
Raleigh	*Where are you going now?*
Kurt	On to the mercantile store.
Raleigh	*Why?*
Kurt	To see the new items that just come in.

Raleigh	*Have you ever been on a ship?*
Kurt	Not a big one, not with sails.
Raleigh	*It wasn't a sail ship?*
Kurt	No.
Raleigh	*What does Albert call you?*
Kurt	Ereekee.
Raleigh	*Ereekee? Say it as he says it.*
Kurt	Ereek.
Raleigh	*Do you have a last name, Eric?*
Kurt	[Long pause.] Ponzel.
Raleigh	*Ponzel?*
Kurt	I can hear my mom calling me that.
Raleigh	*So you could hear your mother calling you Eric Ponzel. Is that correct?*
Kurt	Yes.
Raleigh	*What do people call your mother?*
Kurt	… [Inaudible.]
Raleigh	*Let's go back to the mercantile. Did anything interesting come in?*
Kurt	No, it's still too early to tell, just barrels.
Raleigh	*Were the horses on the ship?*
Kurt	No.
Raleigh	*What year is it right now? Can you see anything with the year on it?*
Kurt	1593, but I'm not sure.
Raleigh	*Why couldn't it be 1593?*
Kurt	It's an amount or number written on a ledger.
Raleigh	*Do you see anything else?*
Kurt	Yes.
Raleigh	*What did you see?*
Kurt	It's a big book, a ledger with beautiful printing in it.

Raleigh	*Yes, so what did it say?*
Kurt	Just keeping track of what was being sold to who and for how much.
Raleigh	*Okay, pick out one of the articles in there and tell me about it.*
Kurt	Black powder.
Raleigh	*Sold to who and for how much?*
Kurt	I can't see that much.
Raleigh	*What town do you live in? I presume you live in a town.*
Kurt	Norgen.
Raleigh	*Okay, Norgen is the town? And what country is that?*
Kurt	Norway.
Raleigh	*Are you happy?*
Kurt	Yes.
Raleigh	*I asked you earlier, but is Albert's family well-to-do or poor?*
Kurt	Well-to-do.
Raleigh	*What does your father do?*
Kurt	A ship captain.
Raleigh	*Do you know what ship he is the captain of? Did you ever see it?*
Kurt	I'm looking for it. I don't see it.
Raleigh	*Did your mom ever see it?*
Kurt	Yes.
Raleigh	*Let's go to that time. What did she say?*
Kurt	"Your father is a great sea captain. He provides our needs. You will do as he says."
Raleigh	*Did you do something wrong?*
Kurt	I don't know. I must have, by the tone of her voice.
Raleigh	*Ha-ha, okay, but what was the name of the ship? What is she telling you?*
Kurt	She's yelling at me.

Raleigh	*What did you do wrong?*
Kurt	I'm not sure, but she is saying, "Wait until your father gets home."
Raleigh	*She said, "Wait until your father gets home"?*
Kurt	Yes. "He'll have a bone to pick with you."
Raleigh	*Did your mom try to swat you?*
Kurt	No, just yell.
Raleigh	*What does your mom look like?*
Kurt	Long dress, hair up in a bun with a hat on it.
Raleigh	*Is she heavy, thin, tall, short, what?*
Kurt	Thin and short.
Raleigh	*Do you have servants?*
Kurt	No.
Raleigh	*Did she ever in this conversation tell you which ship your father is on?*
Kurt	A couple of times, but all I hear is the screaming.
Raleigh	*Okay, let's go to a little bit better time. Do you have brothers or sisters?*
Kurt	Yes, a brother.
Raleigh	*No sisters?*
Kurt	No.
Raleigh	*Just one brother?*
Kurt	Yes.
Raleigh	*Okay, what is his name?*
Kurt	Talon.
Raleigh	*Talon? Okay, is he older than you?*
Kurt	Younger.
Raleigh	*Do you get along with your brother?*
Kurt	For the most part.
Raleigh	*What does he do that you don't like? Something that really makes you mad.*

Kurt   He puts bird poop … puts it on a stick and flings it at me.

Raleigh   *Ha-ha-ha. What do you do when he does that?*

Kurt   Chase him down and tackle him.

Raleigh   *Have you ever done that to him?*

Kurt   Maybe.

Raleigh   *Oh, so is that where he got it?*

Kurt   Could be.

Raleigh   *So, what you are trying to tell me is that you are kind of an ornery kind of little guy?*

Kurt   Could be.

Raleigh   *Do you ever see your dad?*

Kurt   Few and far between.

Raleigh   *What kind of man is he?*

Kurt   Stern.

Raleigh   *Do you like him?*

Kurt   I respect him. He is serious all the time.

Raleigh   *Do you ever see him not serious?*

Kurt   When he's around Mom.

Raleigh   *Are you happy now?*

Kurt   Sometimes.

Raleigh   *Does he ever do anything to you that you like?*

Kurt   When he goes away.

Raleigh   *So when he's around you have to be pretty good?*

Kurt   Oh, yes!

Raleigh   *Does your mother ever tell on you and your brother to get you into trouble?*

Kurt   She threatens but never does.

Raleigh   *Alright, and you are nine years old, correct?*

Kurt   Yes.

Raleigh   *Now let's go up to a pleasant time in your life when you are 12. What do you see?*

Kurt	A hat.
Raleigh	*A hat? What about the hat?*
Kurt	It's clean. It has a feather on it.
Raleigh	*Where is this hat?*
Kurt	On my head.
Raleigh	*Okay, and where did you get this hat?*
Kurt	My mom gave it to me.
Raleigh	*Where are you going that you are wearing this fancy hat?*
Kurt	To main street so I can show it off.
Raleigh	*You're going to Main Street so you can show it off?*
Kurt	The main street.
Raleigh	*Is anyone with you?*
Kurt	No.
Raleigh	*Where did the hat come from?*
Kurt	My mom got it.
Raleigh	*Did she buy it, or your father bring it home, or what?*
Kurt	She traded some sewing for it.
Raleigh	*So your mom sews, too? Is she good?*
Kurt	People think so.
Raleigh	*So she got this hat. Why a hat for you?*
Kurt	A hat makes the man.
Raleigh	*A hat makes the man? Is that how people view it?*
Kurt	It gives you personality.
Raleigh	*What color is it?*
Kurt	Brown.
Raleigh	*Brown hat. What color is the feather?*
Kurt	Brown and white.
Raleigh	*Okay, so it was a pretty nice hat. Has anyone else got a hat like it?*
Kurt	No.
Raleigh	*No? None of your friends?*

Kurt	No, none of my friends.
Raleigh	*What do they say when they see this hat?*
Kurt	Ha-ha, they call me Captain Eric.
Raleigh	*Captain Eric. How are they saying your name while they are doing this?*
Kurt	Ereek.
Raleigh	*Is this Albert doing this?*
Kurt	Yes.
Raleigh	*So you're still friends?*
Kurt	Yes.
Raleigh	*Is he your best friend?*
Kurt	Yes.
Raleigh	*Okay, so it looks like a captain's hat?*
Kurt	No.
Raleigh	*What did you say when he said Captain Eric?*
Kurt	I took off my hat and tipped it to him and said, "Mind your way, sir."
Raleigh	*Ha-ha, what did he say?*
Kurt	He just bowed and let me pass.
Raleigh	*Does this hat have points to the side?*
Kurt	No, front and back.
Raleigh	*Are you going any place in particular?*
Kurt	No, just going to show it off.
Raleigh	*Did the girls like the hat?*
Kurt	They giggled.
Raleigh	*What ever happened to the hat?*
Kurt	It got ran over by a wagon.
Raleigh	*It got ran over by a wagon? Did this happen all in the same year?*
Kurt	No.
Raleigh	*Sometime later?*
Kurt	Sometime.

Raleigh	*And this was the end of the hat?*
Kurt	No, but it just wasn't quite the same after that.
Raleigh	*Alright, but you were still wearing it?*
Kurt	Yes.
Raleigh	*And you still felt the way "it made the man"?*
Kurt	Yes.
Raleigh	*What did you think when it got ran over?*
Kurt	I couldn't believe it. It was like there goes my whole life being crushed.
Raleigh	*Ha-ha.*
Kurt	NOW WHAT?
Raleigh	*You didn't think you could get another hat?*
Kurt	No.
Raleigh	*Was a hat expensive?*
Kurt	I guess I never tried to buy one.
Raleigh	*Did you ever try to go to any type of school?*
Kurt	My mom taught me.
Raleigh	*And what did she teach you?*
Kurt	Stables and horses, how to feed the animals.
Raleigh	*Could your mom read and write?*
Kurt	I don't think so.
Raleigh	*Could you read or write?*
Kurt	No.
Raleigh	*What about your father?*
Kurt	Yes.
Raleigh	*But he never taught you?*
Kurt	He wasn't around.
Raleigh	*Let's continue on.*
Kurt	Alright.
Raleigh	*Let's go to a pleasant time in your life when you are 16. That's a good time in a man's life, 16. You're probably looking at the girls. What do you see?*

Kurt	Gwen.
Raleigh	*Gwen? Okay, is this a girl in your town?*
Kurt	Yes.
Raleigh	*What about Gwen?*
Kurt	She's beautiful.
Raleigh	*Beautiful, okay, tell me about her.*
Kurt	Rosy cheeks with a little bit of freckles, straight long hair.
Raleigh	*What color?*
Kurt	Brunette.
Raleigh	*Brunette, okay.*
Kurt	In braids.
Raleigh	*Is she fat, thin, tall, short?*
Kurt	Thin.
Raleigh	*Is she tall or short?*
Kurt	Tall for her age.
Raleigh	*And you like her a lot?*
Kurt	Yes.
Raleigh	*Does she like you?*
Kurt	I think so.
Raleigh	*You don't know?*
Kurt	No.
Raleigh	*Why not?*
Kurt	I'm too shy.
Raleigh	*Do you ever go over and talk to her?*
Kurt	Oh, no.
Raleigh	*Was this kind of a romance from a distance?*
Kurt	Yes.
Raleigh	*Did you ever go up and tell her how you felt?*
Kurt	No.
Raleigh	*Was this the only girl you ever cared for?*
Kurt	Yes, besides my mom.

Raleigh	*Did you ever tell Albert how you felt about her?*
Kurt	Once.
Raleigh	*What did he say?*
Kurt	Mainly listened.
Raleigh	*He never gave you any advice?*
Kurt	He tried, but I was still too shy.
Raleigh	*Did he have a girlfriend?*
Kurt	Yes.
Raleigh	*What was Albert's girlfriend's name?*
Kurt	Alicia.
Raleigh	*Was she as pretty as Gwen?*
Kurt	Pretty nice.
Raleigh	*Did he ever tell her how he felt?*
Kurt	Yes.
Raleigh	*He did? What did she say about that?*
Kurt	She liked it.
Raleigh	*But you were still too shy?*
Kurt	Yes.
Raleigh	*At 16 you are old enough to see what ship your father was on, correct?*
Kurt	Yes.
Raleigh	*What was the name of that ship?*
Kurt	I can't tell if it's *Theadora* or a *Peadora*.
Raleigh	*You saw it?*
Kurt	No, heard the name. It could be *Veabora*.
Raleigh	*Who said it?*
Kurt	I don't know, a strange voice.
Raleigh	*You never watched your father's ship sail off?*
Kurt	Oh, yes.
Raleigh	*Was the name on the ship?*
Kurt	Yes, I can't get that close to it. I can't read.

Raleigh	*Picture that name of the ship and tell me when you have done that.*
Kurt	Okay.
Raleigh	*Now, remember that name and we will talk about it later. Okay?*
Kurt	Okay.
Raleigh	*What are you wanting to do with your life at 16?*
Kurt	I'm thinking about going to sea.
Raleigh	*Is that what you want to do?*
Kurt	There's not much else to do.
Raleigh	*If you had your choice of doing anything, what would it be? Not because you have to, but because that's what you want to do?*
Kurt	Trade horses.
Raleigh	*Trade horses, so you like horses?*
Kurt	Yes.
Raleigh	*Do you have a job now?*
Kurt	Yes.
Raleigh	*What do you do?*
Kurt	I sweep.
Raleigh	*You sweep, for who?*
Kurt	I am sweeping feathers.
Raleigh	*Sweeping feathers?*
Kurt	At the butcher's.
Raleigh	*What does Albert do?*
Kurt	I don't know.
Raleigh	*You are old enough to see ledgers in the butcher shop or wherever. What year is it now?*
Kurt	I'm walking over there.
Raleigh	*Okay, what do you see?*
Kurt	I don't.
Raleigh	*Was the ledger open?*

Kurt	Yes, I'm trying, but I can't see.
Raleigh	*Okay, have you ever heard anyone speaking about the year?*
Kurt	1608.
Raleigh	*1608, okay, and who said that?*
Kurt	Albert.
Raleigh	*Why did Albert say that?*
Kurt	He was told.
Raleigh	*Could Albert read?*
Kurt	No, but he was told.
Raleigh	*Because your father could read and write, was he considered an influential man?*
Kurt	Yes.
Raleigh	*Okay, what did you normally eat? What was your favorite food?*
Kurt	Biscuits and soup.
Raleigh	*Was that your favorite?*
Kurt	Chicken was good.
Raleigh	*What kind of soup would you have?*
Kurt	Vegetable.
Raleigh	*Did you eat that a lot?*
Kurt	Yes.
Raleigh	*Chicken wasn't as often?*
Kurt	Not as often as I would like.
Raleigh	*Let's go once more, this time to a pleasant time, when you were 20. What do you see?*
Kurt	Water and a sail.
Raleigh	*Where are you at?*
Kurt	I'm on the deck.
Raleigh	*What is your job?*
Kurt	Lookout.
Raleigh	*Lookout?*

Kurt	One of them.
Raleigh	*Are you on the back or the front of the boat?*
Kurt	On the front.
Raleigh	*Are you seeing anything?*
Kurt	I'm not on duty.
Raleigh	*Okay, so are you just looking around?*
Kurt	Swabbing the deck.
Raleigh	*So, when you're not on duty, you're swabbing the deck.*
Kurt	I know.
Raleigh	*Do you have any free time to relax?*
Kurt	Only when sleeping.
Raleigh	*Is anyone with you while swabbing the deck?*
Kurt	Four or five.
Raleigh	*Is Albert on the ship with you?*
Kurt	No.
Raleigh	*Where is he?*
Kurt	He's trading horses.
Raleigh	*The job you wanted to do? There's something not quite right about that, is there?*
Kurt	Huh, he should be here.
Raleigh	*What do you think about the sea?*
Kurt	Powerful and tranquil.
Raleigh	*Why did you decide to go to the sea?*
Kurt	The adventure.
Raleigh	*Have you seen adventure already?*
Kurt	Yes.
Raleigh	*In what form?*
Kurt	Big ships going by in the ports.
Raleigh	*What is the most favorite place you went?*
Kurt	Carthage.
Raleigh	*What made that so special?*
Kurt	It's beautiful.

Raleigh *Who was your captain?*

Kurt Bela Docker.

Raleigh *Was he from Norway?*

Kurt I believe he was.

Raleigh *Did he speak the same language as you?*

Kurt Yes.

Raleigh *Was there anything about the ship you didn't like?*

Kurt Cold, wet, rats, food, smell, sometimes small, sometimes real big at others.

Raleigh *So there wasn't too much you really did like?*

Kurt The sound of the wind in the sails.

Raleigh *Can you swim?*

Kurt Yes.

Raleigh *Have you ever thought of doing something else?*

Kurt From time to time. The sea has a good pull.

Raleigh *Let's go up in time again. Did you ever have times in
which you were afraid?*

Kurt Yes.

Raleigh *And what was that?*

Kurt The time we were broadsided.

Raleigh *Broadsided, okay. How far away were you?*

Kurt Too darn close. I would say 600 knots, no, 300
knots.

Raleigh *How long are you calling a knot?*

Kurt It's just a distance. I can't hardly spread my arms
this far.

Raleigh *By spreading both arms you can almost touch it?*

Kurt Yes, almost.

Raleigh *So was 300 knots close for broadsiding?*

Kurt No, I don't think they wanted to sink us. They just
wanted to scare the shit out of us. The cannon were
falling short, but there was one that smacked us.

Raleigh	*Were you scared?*
Kurt	Oh, oh, oh, I don't think anyone wasn't!
Raleigh	*Do you have cannons?*
Kurt	No.
Raleigh	*So you couldn't even fire back?*
Kurt	We could outrun it though.
Raleigh	*Were they after you?*
Kurt	We just got too close to their territory.
Raleigh	*Was this like a battleship?*
Kurt	Yes.
Raleigh	*What nationality?*
Kurt	It looks like Portuguese.
Raleigh	*Is this because of the flag?*
Kurt	No, by what is being said.
Raleigh	*Who is saying this?*
Kurt	A lot of the men on board.
Raleigh	*Does it look different than yours?*
Kurt	Oh, yeah.
Raleigh	*Is it larger than yours?*
Kurt	We have larger sails.
Raleigh	*Are they still chasing you?*
Kurt	No.
Raleigh	*Did you ever have any more close calls like that?*
Kurt	No.
Raleigh	*You say one cannonball did hit the ship. Did it do much damage?*
Kurt	It hit on midship right above the deck and blew the railing off, went to the other side, and blew part of the railing off.
Raleigh	*Let's continue on. You're age 20 now, correct?*
Kurt	Yes.
Raleigh	*Did you see age 25?*

Kurt	No.
Raleigh	*Did you see age 24?*
Kurt	No.
Raleigh	*Did you see age 23?*
Kurt	Yes.
Raleigh	*Did you ever settle down and take a wife?*
Kurt	No.
Raleigh	*Did you ever change jobs?*
Kurt	No.
Raleigh	*Are you still on the* Annabella? *[From a previous session.]*
Kurt	Yes.
Raleigh	*Is it still the same captain?*
Kurt	Yes.
Raleigh	*Do you ever take shore leave at all?*
Kurt	Whenever we deliver into port.
Raleigh	*Do you ever go back home much?*
Kurt	From time to time.
Raleigh	*Do you go see your mom?*
Kurt	Yes.
Raleigh	*Do you see your dad?*
Kurt	He's never around.
Raleigh	*Do you ever see him in different ports?*
Kurt	No.
Raleigh	*What is your job on ship now?*
Kurt	Still lookout.
Raleigh	*Do you like that job?*
Kurt	Yes.
Raleigh	*Have you ever been offered promotions?*
Kurt	No.
Raleigh	*How much do you get paid?*
Kurt	Five ducats per month.

Raleigh	*A ducat? How much is a ducat worth?*
Kurt	It's a ducat.
Raleigh	*Okay, let's put it this way, what would one ducat buy?*
Kurt	A barrel of wine.
Raleigh	*A barrel of wine?*
Kurt	No, a BARREL of wine.
Raleigh	*Well, just how much wine is this?*
Kurt	Enough to get the crew drunk for a week.
Raleigh	*Do you have friends on the ship?*
Kurt	The cook.
Raleigh	*Tell me about the cook.*
Kurt	He's got a beard, a nice guy.
Raleigh	*Is he from Norway, as well?*
Kurt	I don't think so.
Raleigh	*What makes you think that?*
Kurt	He has an accent.
Raleigh	*If he has an accent, how does he call you?*
Kurt	Orick, that's close but not quite. He's trying to say "E" but can't quite.
Raleigh	*What do you call him?*
Kurt	Ah, Gushy.
Raleigh	*And what does that stand for?*
Kurt	Gustoff, he's the cook.
Raleigh	*What is the best thing he can cook?*
Kurt	Sea bass.
Raleigh	*What's the worst thing that he cooks?*
Kurt	Everything else.
Raleigh	*Ha-ha, so he is a pretty lousy cook.*
Kurt	Oh, he's pretty good. We tease him all the time.
Raleigh	*What do you mainly eat on the ship?*
Kurt	Fish and biscuits.
Raleigh	*Is it normally fresh fish you catch?*

Kurt	Yes.
Raleigh	*Do you catch the fish?*
Kurt	Occasionally.
Raleigh	*You're just a cargo ship, right?*
Kurt	Yes.
Raleigh	*Do you see gold or silver come on board?*
Kurt	We took some passengers on, and they had gold.
Raleigh	*Where did you take the passengers to?*
Kurt	Sweden.
Raleigh	*Did the cook fix the same food for the passengers that he did for you?*
Kurt	Nooo.
Raleigh	*What would he cook passengers?*
Kurt	Whatever the captain was having.
Raleigh	*Oh, so the captain wouldn't eat the same food? What would he eat?*
Kurt	Something better than what we ate. I don't know. I wasn't privy to that. But Gustoff said it would just make me fat thinking about it.
Raleigh	*Did he ever let you taste what the captain ate?*
Kurt	No.
Raleigh	*The captain was the only one who ate it?*
Kurt	No, he had his officers.
Raleigh	*How many people were on your ship?*
Kurt	Thirty-five.
Raleigh	*So, how many officers did you have?*
Kurt	Two.
Raleigh	*The men must have been pretty obedient with only two officers and the captain.*
Kurt	Yes.
Raleigh	*Was the captain a good captain?*
Kurt	He was fair.

Raleigh *You, being the ornery young man that you were, did you ever get into trouble?*

Kurt There wasn't time.

Raleigh *Let's come to the time you said you didn't get past 23. What happened then?*

Kurt I was tethering the sail and fell off.

Raleigh *Were you at sea?*

Kurt Yes.

Raleigh *Did anyone see this?*

Kurt Half of the crew.

Raleigh *When you fell off, what happened?*

Kurt I landed on my back over the railing, fell overboard.

Raleigh *Did you break your back?*

Kurt I think so.

Raleigh *Can you move your legs?*

Kurt No.

Raleigh *Did you fall into the ocean?*

Kurt Yes.

Raleigh *Did you drown?*

Kurt Yes.

Raleigh *Did the ship come back and get you?*

Kurt They tried, but it was too late.

Raleigh *So they never retrieved your body?*

Kurt No.

Raleigh *What happened after that?*

Kurt I rose out of the water, went past the sails, and went into the sun.

Raleigh *Was this something you felt you had to do?*

Kurt No.

Raleigh *Did you know what was happening?*

Kurt I know I wasn't hurting anymore.

Raleigh *Were you still conscious of yourself?*

Kurt	Yes, it was as natural as could be.
Raleigh	*Where did you go after you went into the sun?*
Kurt	I met Jesus.
Raleigh	*You met Jesus? Immediately? Look at yourself. How are you clothed?*
Kurt	I can't see.
Raleigh	*Okay, is Jesus in front of you?*
Kurt	Yes.
Raleigh	*What does He look like?*
Kurt	Very bright, His clothes are bright.
Raleigh	*Were you, as a child, taught about Jesus?*
Kurt	Yes.
Raleigh	*Is He as you pictured Him?*
Kurt	No.
Raleigh	*What did you think He would look like?*
Kurt	Like a captain.
Raleigh	*You mean like being stern?*
Kurt	Full of command.
Raleigh	*And how do you find Him?*
Kurt	Still in command, but gentle.
Raleigh	*Would you have imagined His appearance to look like this?*
Kurt	No.
Raleigh	*How would you have pictured Him? Let me put it this way, what is very surprising to you?*
Kurt	How tall He is.
Raleigh	*How tall is that?*
Kurt	Six foot four.
Raleigh	*Big build, small build, what?*
Kurt	Pretty good-sized.
Raleigh	*Is He talking to you?*
Kurt	With His eyes.

Raleigh	*What color are they?*
Kurt	Blue.
Raleigh	*What is He telling you with His eyes?*
Kurt	"Welcome home."
Raleigh	*Say exactly what He says.*
Kurt	"Good to see you again. Welcome home."
Raleigh	*Did you say anything?*
Kurt	"Why did it take so long? Why was I gone so long?"
Raleigh	*What did He say?*
Kurt	"You had to learn your lessons."
Raleigh	*Then what did you say?*
Kurt	"Yeah, it takes time to learn lessons."
Raleigh	*What was your lesson to learn?*
Kurt	It's people that matters, where emotions and relationships are involved.
Raleigh	*Did you feel unfulfilled that you never truly learned love?*
Kurt	I loved my mom.
Raleigh	*But what about Gwen? You were never able to show her.*
Kurt	But I loved her.
Raleigh	*What happened next?*
Kurt	I asked, "What do you do up here?"
Raleigh	*What did He say?*
Kurt	"Wonderful things."
Raleigh	*And then what?*
Kurt	He said, "What would you like to do?"
Raleigh	*What did you say?*
Kurt	"To be at Your feet for a while."
Raleigh	*And what did He say?*
Kurt	"Okay."
Raleigh	*What happened next?*

Kurt	I'm still holding His feet.
Raleigh	*And this is where you want to be?*
Kurt	The best place around.

While under hypnosis, Kurt drew the symbol Eric used as his signature on the *Annabella*. It was an oar with three slashes across the handle.

A few days later when I was in Atlanta on business, I received a call from a very excited Kurt. He told me he had been researching the information from his session. He found a ship, the *Annabella,* which was named after her owner's wife. Kurt was also excited to report that the currency of the day was the ducat.

EPISODE 4

◆ A Brick Wall ◆

EDWARD AND I met many years ago and became instant friends. I gave him a copy of one of my missing-person sessions, and he was fascinated with our work. He was a regular participant until he got married and moved. He is now a minister in Texas.

This story, although very profound, has to be one of the saddest. It shows how cruel and intolerant people can truly be.

Raleigh	*We are now going to another time, another place before you were born. A place you know nothing of. What do you see?*
Edward	It looks like a wall.
Raleigh	*Okay, tell me about the wall.*
Edward	It's like I have my face smashed up against a brick wall.
Raleigh	*Your face is smashed against a brick wall?*
Edward	Yeah.
Raleigh	*Okay, describe the person you are seeing.*
Edward	I don't see anything other than a brick wall.
Raleigh	*Alright, what else is around this wall? Anything?*
Edward	I don't see anything.
Raleigh	*Do you feel the wall?*
Edward	Yes.
Raleigh	*Yes?*
Edward	Yes, the mortar is cutting my nose.

Raleigh	*Do you feel any other pressure on your body other than the wall?*
Edward	Yes.
Raleigh	*From behind?*
Edward	Yes.
Raleigh	*What is causing that pressure?*
Edward	I don't know.
Raleigh	*Alright, let's back up into time a little farther. Do you understand?*
Edward	Yes.
Raleigh	*Tell me what you see now. We are no longer at the wall. We are going back before that time.*
Edward	I'm in a wagon.
Raleigh	*You're in a wagon?*
Edward	Laying down.
Raleigh	*You're in the back of the wagon?*
Edward	Yes.
Raleigh	*What kind of a wagon is it?*
Edward	Very thin, big wheels. When I look up, there is a piece of wood. The man is leaning back on it. He has on a fuzzy hat.
Raleigh	*A fuzzy hat?*
Edward	Yes.
Raleigh	*Fuzzy as in fur?*
Edward	I don't know. Black. It might be round. I don't know what it is made of. Fuzzy.
Raleigh	*Do you know that man?*
Edward	I can't see him.
Raleigh	*Okay, can you see yourself?*
Edward	No.
Raleigh	*Alright, are you merely relaxing or have you been injured?*

Edward	I'm hurt. I'm looking up at the trees. I can't move. I can't sit up.
Raleigh	*Okay, let's go back before that point. Understand?*
Edward	Yes.
Raleigh	*We are going back further up the trail. Okay?*
Edward	Yeah.
Raleigh	*This is before the wagon. What are you doing before the wagon?*
Edward	I see a field and a plow.
Raleigh	*A field and a plow?*
Edward	Yeah.
Raleigh	*Where are you in relation to that?*
Edward	Just standing in the field looking at the plow.
Raleigh	*How old are you?*
Edward	Thirty maybe.
Raleigh	*Thirty maybe? Okay, describe yourself to me. What do you look like?*
Edward	Thin, wearing rags.
Raleigh	*Wearing rags?*
Edward	Yes. Very thin hair.
Raleigh	*Thin hair. What color?*
Edward	Brown.
Raleigh	*Okay, what is your name?*
Edward	I don't know.
Raleigh	*No problem. Do you live near this field? [Pause.] What are the thoughts going through your head as you are standing in this field?*
Edward	I'm not very smart.
Raleigh	*You're not very smart?*
Edward	No.
Raleigh	*Okay, but you still have thoughts.*
Edward	I want to plow.

Raleigh	*You want to plow?*
Edward	Yeah.
Raleigh	*Do you know how to plow?*
Edward	No.
Raleigh	*When you say you are not very smart, does that mean you are less smart than most people?*
Edward	Yes.
Raleigh	*Is that because you have not had schooling or because you were born that way?*
Edward	I was born.
Raleigh	*You were born that way, okay. When people speak to you, do you normally know what they are saying?*
Edward	No, they don't talk to me very often.
Raleigh	*Do you understand what I am saying?*
Edward	Yes.
Raleigh	*Are you afraid to talk to me?*
Edward	Yes.
Raleigh	*Why?*
Edward	Nobody ever talked to me before.
Raleigh	*Okay, you don't need to be afraid of me. Okay?*
Edward	Okay.
Raleigh	*What do people call you for a name? I refer to not as a mean name, but when people call you by name. What do people call you?*
Edward	Anthony.
Raleigh	*Anthony, okay. Anthony, do you have a home nearby?*
Edward	No.
Raleigh	*Where did you come from?*
Edward	The river.
Raleigh	*The river?*
Edward	Yes.
Raleigh	*Do you have a home on the river?*

Edward	No.
Raleigh	*Do you have a family on the river?*
Edward	No.
Raleigh	*Were you lost?*
Edward	I don't know.
Raleigh	*Where did you come from, on the river?*
Edward	Yes.
Raleigh	*Any particular place?*
Edward	It was a good place to sleep, right next to the trees.
Raleigh	*Okay, let's go back farther in your life. Okay, Anthony? Let's go back to when you had a family. Do you understand?*
Edward	Yes.
Raleigh	*At one point in your life you had a family. We are going back to those times. Do you understand?*
Edward	I was very young.
Raleigh	*You were very young?*
Edward	Yes.
Raleigh	*Tell me about your family.*
Edward	They're … they're poor. They were poor, and they took me to another woman. They leave.
Raleigh	*You leave with the other woman. Is that correct?*
Edward	No, no. I stay with the other woman.
Raleigh	*Who left you — the mother or the father?*
Edward	My mother.
Raleigh	*Your mother. Did she call you Anthony?*
Edward	She didn't say anything.
Raleigh	*Alright, what did the other people say to you?*
Edward	Nothing.
Raleigh	*Okay, how old were you?*
Edward	A baby.
Raleigh	*A baby?*

Edward	Yeah.
Raleigh	*Okay, as in a very small baby?*
Edward	I was walking.
Raleigh	*You were walking, but you were still pretty small. Maybe one?*
Edward	Maybe one.
Raleigh	*Okay, these people that took care of you then, were they also poor?*
Edward	Yes.
Raleigh	*Were they nice people?*
Edward	They didn't talk to me.
Raleigh	*Why?*
Edward	I was always on the side. They would talk to each other. They fight.
Raleigh	*They fight? About what?*
Edward	Food, housing, planting … they fight about everything … always fighting.
Raleigh	*They were always fighting?*
Edward	Umm hmm.
Raleigh	*Were there other children there?*
Edward	No.
Raleigh	*You were the only one?*
Edward	Umm hmm.
Raleigh	*When they did come to talk to you, what did they say?*
Edward	"GROW!" That is what he would say.
Raleigh	*The man would say, "Grow"?*
Edward	Umm hmm, he wanted me to work with him. He told me to, "GROW!"
Raleigh	*Alright, time goes by with these people. How long did you stay with these people?*
Edward	He told me to leave!
Raleigh	*How old were you then?*

Edward	Very small.
Raleigh	*Very small? How old?*
Edward	Four, maybe five.
Raleigh	*Okay, why did he tell you to leave?*
Edward	I was stupid. I couldn't do nothin'.
Raleigh	*Did you leave?*
Edward	I had to. He hit me.
Raleigh	*Where did you go?*
Edward	I just ran through the fields. I slept in the grass, then I went to a building and asked for food.
Raleigh	*Did they give you food?*
Edward	I had to sweep.
Raleigh	*You were only four?*
Edward	Yes.
Raleigh	*What country are you in?*
Edward	I don't know.
Raleigh	*Alright, what is the year? [He was having some problems with these questions.]*
Edward	One … seven … four … nine.
Raleigh	*1749, does that seem correct?*
Edward	Yes.
Raleigh	*Was there ever a town that you saw?*
Edward	No, just fields.
Raleigh	*Just fields, alright. Did anyone ever take care of you then?*
Edward	No.
Raleigh	*You were so small!*
Edward	I tried to follow people. I just ate what I could. I had to steal clothes.
Raleigh	*Okay, no one ever wanted to take you in because you were slow?*
Edward	I also walked funny. I kind of drag my right foot.

Raleigh	*Okay, so you had something wrong with your foot?*
Edward	Yes.
Raleigh	*What was wrong with your foot?*
Edward	It kind of turned sideways. It just sort of hung there.
Raleigh	*Alright, how old are you now … then?*
Edward	Umm … 13, maybe.
Raleigh	*What is your view of life?*
Edward	Stay warm, get some food.
Raleigh	*So you are just by yourself?*
Edward	Yes.
Raleigh	*Have you ever had any friends?*
Edward	Only one small boy.
Raleigh	*One small boy.*
Edward	His dad said, "No!"
Raleigh	*No about what?*
Edward	No, that I couldn't stay with them, that I was a monster. He said, "No, he's got a disease."
Raleigh	*Did you have a disease?*
Edward	I don't know ….
Raleigh	*Okay. As far as you know, there was nothing else wrong, other than your leg and that you weren't very smart.*
Edward	Not that I know of.
Raleigh	*The people that are speaking to you, do their voices sound like mine?*
Edward	No.
Raleigh	*What's different?*
Edward	They're all angry.
Raleigh	*Okay, other than the tone of their voice, it's the same language?*
Edward	I … I can't talk. I don't know.
Raleigh	*Alright.*

Edward	I can't talk.
Raleigh	*Why can't you talk?*
Edward	I … don't hear. I … don't hear. I can't talk, and I don't hear.
Raleigh	*You can't talk, and you don't hear?*
Edward	Yes.
Raleigh	*Okay, and you have a bad foot. Those are the things that are wrong with you?*
Edward	I … don't know what most things are.
Raleigh	*Is it pleasurable for you to be able to speak to me now?*
Edward	Yes.
Raleigh	*You can express yourself, and you can speak to me.*
Edward	You mean I can think?
Raleigh	*Yes, you can.*
Edward	I know what I've seen. I saw it was a plow. I didn't know it was a plow.
Raleigh	*Okay, do you feel better about that? You're not dumb, are you?*
Edward	No. I … I … just didn't know everything was … just … they would point. I … I didn't know what they wanted. I just didn't know. I … I can't tell, "It doesn't help to just point."
Raleigh	*Do you ever get angry or frustrated because of this?*
Edward	No! I get scared because they would hit me.
Raleigh	*Could you make any sounds for people to understand you?*
Edward	I … I could put my hand out in front of me. I tried.
Raleigh	*Alright, that must have been very hard. How did you make friends with the boy, then?*

Edward	He has no friends. I hold my hand out, and he would give me some food. He would hold my hand and would pull me to his house.
Raleigh	*He was a nice boy, then?*
Edward	Yes, he would break me off some bread. He was a very nice boy.
Raleigh	*Alright, you grew to be a man, and it must have been very hard. You lived your life all that way. Did you have any more friends?*
Edward	Animals.
Raleigh	*Animals?*
Edward	Horses.
Raleigh	*How did you get to this place, where the field and plow were?*
Edward	I just walked.
Raleigh	*Were you always within the same area all your life?*
Edward	Always fields.
Raleigh	*What I mean … were these the same people and fields you saw as a child?*
Edward	I … I had to go. The same people everywhere … always hitting and hurting me.
Raleigh	*Everywhere you went, people were the same way?*
Edward	It was like they were all scared of me.
Raleigh	*Alright, what happened that this man had you in this wagon?*
Edward	He hit me.
Raleigh	*He hit you? Why?*
Edward	With the surrey.
Raleigh	*Oh, he hit you with the wagon. Where were you?*
Edward	Coming out of trees. I couldn't hear him.
Raleigh	*Okay, I can understand that. What did the man do then?*

Edward   I turned and looked at him. He didn't even try to stop.

Raleigh   *Don't feel, just tell me what happened.*

Edward   I got hit by the front where you hook the horses on, and the wheels rolled over me.

Raleigh   *Was it an empty wagon?*

Edward   I don't know.

Raleigh   *Was the wagon going fast?*

Edward   No, not really.

Raleigh   *Did the man stop?*

Edward   Yes.

Raleigh   *What did he do then?*

Edward   Yelling at me. I couldn't do anything.

Raleigh   *Were you on the ground?*

Edward   Yes.

Raleigh   *Were you hurt badly?*

Edward   Yes.

Raleigh   *Did the man help you then?*

Edward   The man is lifting my head up and plopped it back down. My head was open.

Raleigh   *Your head was open?*

Edward   Yes.

Raleigh   *You mean like a cut?*

Edward   Worse, like a hole right next to my ear.

Raleigh   *The part about the wall you told me about, was that before or after the part about the wagon?*

Edward   After.

Raleigh   *So, did you live past this accident?*

Edward   I don't know.

Raleigh   *Let's continue on. You had a hole in your head.*

Edward   Yes.

Raleigh   *What did the man do then?*

Edward	He put me in the wagon.
Raleigh	*Although you couldn't hear him then, you now can. What was the man saying to you after he hit you?*
Edward	"You stupid, vhy ver you in da road? What ver you doing in da road? I have to hit you. I cannot stop. Vhy ver you in da road? Vhat ver you doing in da road? Now look at you, are you alive or not?" [Spoken in a Dutch accent.]
Raleigh	*Is this when he lifted your head up?*
Edward	Yes.
Raleigh	*How is this man dressed?*
Edward	White shirt, very long sleeves, cuffs doubled up. Black pants. Black vest.
Raleigh	*Okay, you were in the wagon. Let's go to the end of that journey. Okay?*
Edward	Yes.
Raleigh	*Where did the man take you?*
Edward	I see trees, sky. He picks me up and lays me on the ground.
Raleigh	*Okay, did he think you were dead?*
Edward	Yes.
Raleigh	*What did he say to you then?*
Edward	"Dat vould be good enough for you until I get somebody." [Dutch accent.] There are bricks.
Raleigh	*What about the bricks?*
Edward	They are on my nose.
Raleigh	*Bricks on your nose?*
Edward	They were cutting me where he threw me down.
Raleigh	*Oh! It wasn't a wall; it was like a street.*
Edward	Yes.
Raleigh	*So you were laying face down.*
Edward	Yes.

Raleigh	*What was holding you down?*
Edward	I cannot move.
Raleigh	*Is this because you were hurt too bad?*
Edward	I'm almost dead.
Raleigh	*You were almost dead? Do you hear people around you?*
Edward	No.
Raleigh	*Now you can hear. Is anyone around you?*
Edward	A man.
Raleigh	*What is he saying now?*
Edward	"You dumb kid, now I have to get somebody."
Raleigh	*Who is he talking to?*
Edward	I don't know.
Raleigh	*Did anyone answer him?*
Edward	I don't know.
Raleigh	*But you were close to being dead, correct?*
Edward	Yes.
Raleigh	*Did anyone return?*
Edward	I don't ....
Raleigh	*Did you live past this day?*
Edward	No.
Raleigh	*You did die that day?*
Edward	Yes.
Raleigh	*Are you afraid of me?*
Edward	Yes, some.
Raleigh	*Why?*
Edward	I can hear you and talk to you. I never have.
Raleigh	*I'm not here to hurt you. Did you ever see the man and woman who threw you out when you were so young?*
Edward	No.
Raleigh	*We are going to continue on. What happened after you died? Tell me what you saw.*
Edward	I never seen ....

Raleigh	*Tell me what you see.*
Edward	Light and dark both. I feel very comfortable.
Raleigh	*Are you in the light?*
Edward	Yes, it's very bright. It's right in front of me.
Raleigh	*Tell me when you meet someone.*
Edward	A man.
Raleigh	*What does he look like?*
Edward	Bigger than me.
Raleigh	*How much is bigger?*
Edward	Maybe twice my size. I am very humble.
Raleigh	*How is this individual dressed?*
Edward	Very, very, very white. I dare not look. I'm humble. He says, "I am your Creator. I am God. I am so glad you are here and you can understand."
Raleigh	*Were you scared then?*
Edward	No.
Raleigh	*What else were you told?*
Edward	"Your suffering is over, My child. Come live in peace."
Raleigh	*Are you still there?*
Edward	Yes, still there.

EPISODE 5

◆ A Pyramid ◆

WHEN I MET Janet, I was giving a lecture in Wichita, Kansas. Her life is similar to most of ours. She works in a factory, has a daughter, goes to college, and is trying to better her life.

I never know what will be the result of these sessions; but after 30 years, I never cease to be amazed. Janet went to sleep quite easily, and soon we had gone through her life and into the previous life.

Janet is very dedicated to the work I do in finding lost people. We have gotten together several times. Each session is just as interesting as the first, and each question I ask leads to five more.

We are now about to embark on a long and distant journey, so make yourself comfortable and enjoy the trip back, back in time. This is her first session.

Raleigh	*You are now going to another time, another place, before you were born. A place you know nothing of. What do you see?*
Janet	I see the sun setting.
Raleigh	*Look all around. What else do you see?*
Janet	Sand.
Raleigh	*Sand, okay, are there trees or anything like that?*
Janet	No, there's a pyramid.
Raleigh	*How far away?*
Janet	You could probably walk to it.

Raleigh	*Just one?*
Janet	Yes.
Raleigh	*Okay, look at yourself. How are you dressed?*
Janet	I have black leather, with silver chains or something around my waist.
Raleigh	*Continue on. Why are you in this area?*
Janet	This is the area they're going to bury me in.
Raleigh	*They are going to bury you here?*
Janet	Yes, it's my pyramid.
Raleigh	*That's your pyramid. Okay, is there anyone with you?*
Janet	Yes, but they're behind me. They have to stay behind.
Raleigh	*How old are you?*
Janet	I was 12 when they started, and I'm 16 now.
Raleigh	*What do people call you?*
Janet	To my face? Ha-ha.
Raleigh	*Yes, to your face.*
Janet	I'm Daddy's Girl.
Raleigh	*You're Daddy's Girl, so people don't talk to you?*
Janet	They have to tell my Lady to talk.
Raleigh	*So they have to talk through others to talk to you. What about Daddy?*
Janet	He just calls me Princess.
Raleigh	*At some time or another you heard your name. Correct? What were you called?*
Janet	I … I can't hear it.
Raleigh	*You can't hear it?*
Janet	My Lady, she knows me.
Raleigh	*She knows you?*
Janet	Yes, she takes me to the stars.
Raleigh	*Let's come up in time, your pyramid is started and you're 16 now. You are alive, correct?*

Janet	Yes.
Raleigh	*Did you see age 20?*
Janet	I never have any children.
Raleigh	*You never have any children. Did you see age 20?*
Janet	I ... I can't.
Raleigh	*Okay, let's come back. Did you see age 17?*
Janet	Yes.
Raleigh	*Did you see age 18?*
Janet	Kind of.
Raleigh	*Part of it, okay. Somewhere in the course of your life either your father or your mother told you what your name was, didn't they?*
Janet	It's right there. I can see it before me. I ... I wear it around my neck.
Raleigh	*Okay, if you would open your eyes, and I shall give you a pencil and paper. Now try and draw what you see.*
Raleigh	*Is this like a necklace for you?*
Janet	It has snakes that protect me. The snakes strike out. They protect me. It says I'm a child of Isis. I am a princess. My tomb is covered with gold.
Raleigh	*Your tomb is covered with gold? You are only going to see it, correct?*
Janet	It's pretty. I have everything.
Raleigh	*What do you think about seeing a place where your body will be placed?*
Janet	It's just my body. The Lady will take me to the stars so I don't have to stay in there.
Raleigh	*You say there is only one pyramid there and it is yours. Is that correct?*
Janet	Yes.
Raleigh	*Have you ever seen others?*

Janet   Yes, but I don't care about them.

Raleigh   *What are you drawing right now?*

Janet   My horse, it will carry me to the stars.

Raleigh   *What else have you drawn?*

Janet   My necklace.

Raleigh   *What is the significance of this necklace?*

Janet   The Lady gave it to me, and the snakes on it will keep me free from harm.

Raleigh   *So your snakes protect you?*

Janet   They are powerful.

Raleigh   *Let's go to a time where your father actually speaks to you. Do you understand? We are going to a time where he actually calls you by name. Understand?*

Janet   Yes, Adelia.

Raleigh   *Adelia?*

Janet   Yes.

Raleigh   *Now, who is your father? What do they call him?*

Janet   He is a big man. He's the King. He's the Pharaoh.

Raleigh   *What do the crowds call him? [She starts to cry.] Why are you sad?*

Janet   They are going to kill him.

Raleigh   *Why?*

Janet   [Sob, sob.] I don't know why that man is mean.

Raleigh   *What country are you in?*

Janet   Egypt, and the Nile River. The river floods.

Raleigh   *It floods?*

Janet   Yes.

Raleigh   *Often?*

Janet   Once a year it floods, once a year.

Raleigh   *Is it the flood time right now?*

Janet	No … no, I don't think so. He just wants to kill him because he's mean. He wants his chair. He wants his pyramid, and he can't have it because my dad is the King. He can't have it! [Sob.]
Raleigh	*He can't have it?*
Janet	No, [sob, sob] but they won't let me go. [Sob.] They won't let me go, [sob] but I know they're going to kill him.
Raleigh	*Where is this man from?*
Janet	My dad thinks that he is his friend. He calls him his friend, but he is not!
Raleigh	*How do you know this is going to happen?*
Janet	You look at him, he plans, he plans. He talks to my dad; he calls him friend. Then behind his back he talks bad about him.
Raleigh	*Have you heard him?*
Janet	Yeah, yeah.
Raleigh	*Who has he told this to?*
Janet	The warriors. They have swords; they have spears.
Raleigh	*What does your dad call this man other than friend?*
Janet	Brother.
Raleigh	*Okay, but he has a real name.*
Janet	Yeah, but it sounds strange.
Raleigh	*Okay, but say it as you hear it.*
Janet	Ruphaul.
Raleigh	*Is he from Egypt as well?*
Janet	Not the same place, not the same city.
Raleigh	*Alright, what does he call your dad? Other than friend, brother, what does he call your dad?*
Janet	I'm listening. I can't hear it.
Raleigh	*Is your mother alive?*
Janet	I am the child of the goddess Isis.

Raleigh	*You are the child of Isis?*
Janet	She protects me.
Raleigh	*What are you doing right now?*
Janet	I'm in a room and the door is shut, but it's not my room.
Raleigh	*Are you talking about this moment in time?*
Janet	No, it's not my room; they took me there. It's so they can hurt my dad and I can't warn him. They want to kill him.
Raleigh	*Then what would they do with you?*
Janet	They know what they are going to do to me.
Raleigh	*Okay, do they plan the same fate for you?*
Janet	Yes.
Raleigh	*Are you afraid?*
Janet	No.
Raleigh	*Then why are you sad for your dad? You know whatever happens to you that you will travel to the stars. Correct?*
Janet	But I have the power given to me by my mother.
Raleigh	*Yes, but your dad is pretty important, too.*
Janet	She marked it, and they will all be sorry.
Raleigh	*What do you mean she marked it?*
Janet	She marked my soul, and when they kill me … and when they kill me … it will be all right.
Raleigh	*Let me get this right. She marked your soul so when they kill you, it will be all right?*
Janet	Yes.
Raleigh	*What do they do when they mark your soul?*
Janet	Isis, she protects me.
Raleigh	*Isis protects you?*
Janet	I have a light, and I have a power to go to the stars.
Raleigh	*You have a light and power to go to the stars?*

Janet	Oh, yeah. They can hurt my physical body, but they can never hurt me.
Raleigh	*They can hurt the physical body, but they can never hurt you. Is that right?*
Janet	Yeah, she will bring my horse, and I will ride to the stars. My body will lie in my pyramid, but my soul will not.
Raleigh	*I want you to let yourself go right now and tell me what year is this. [VERY restless.] Are you calm with yourself?*
Janet	I have so much energy! I can feel my power!
Raleigh	*Okay.*
Janet	I feel my power as my time draws near. It's like my whole body is alive with electricity. I feel so charged! I feel no pain!
Raleigh	*Okay, slow down, stay at my pace, okay?*
Janet	Okay.
Raleigh	*Now, what year is this? And you will have to put it into my time. Understand?*
Janet	Yeah.
Raleigh	*Put it into either B.C. or A.D., and I know you can do that.*
Janet	It was before your Christ.
Raleigh	*Okay, I'm sure of that.*
Janet	It was before your Christ. It is the time of my Christ.
Raleigh	*Which was?*
Janet	He was born of a virgin.
Raleigh	*Are we speaking of Osiris?*
Janet	[Very loud and excited.] Yeah!
Raleigh	*Does this surprise you that I know of him?*
Janet	Don't all know?

Raleigh	*No, they don't.*
Janet	[Deep gasp.] Huh! I'm burning the incense.
Raleigh	*Are you a daughter of Osiris?*
Janet	All of us are a child of God, you choose your heart.
Raleigh	*Okay, but are you physically a daughter of Osiris? If Isis is your mother?*
Janet	Isis protects me.
Raleigh	*Okay, Isis protects, but is she actually your physical mother?*
Janet	I am the Princess; I am the Daughter .... My flesh burns.
Raleigh	*Okay, you said your flesh burns. Let's go back to that. Just tell me about it, don't feel it. I can remove the pain. The pain is gone. You are just telling me what caused the pain.*
Janet	The knife.
Raleigh	*Someone took a knife to you?*
Janet	Yeah, right here. [Indicates center chest.]
Raleigh	*Who did this?*
Janet	A man.
Raleigh	*Have you seen this man before?*
Janet	Yes, near my room, in the hallways.
Raleigh	*Do you know who he is?*
Janet	Yes, he was my father's friend. My uncle.
Raleigh	*Your uncle? So this was really your father's brother?*
Janet	Yes, he will rob my tomb, but he won't find it.
Raleigh	*He won't find your tomb?*
Janet	Yeah, he will, but he won't find what he's looking for.
Raleigh	*What's he looking for?*
Janet	He wants my necklace. He wants my power. He wants to choose life and death.

Raleigh	*Did he ever find your necklace?*
Janet	No, no one finds my necklace.
Raleigh	*So it is still hidden today? I won't try to find it.*
Janet	I know where it is.
Raleigh	*You know your spirit is safe with me.*
Janet	When you look to the east, you will find where my Sorcerer, my Lady, took me to the stars. You will find her; and when I'm in the tomb, don't let them bury her with me.
Raleigh	*Is this the woman who is to take you to the stars?*
Janet	Yes.
Raleigh	*Why?*
Janet	Because she holds my Isis.
Raleigh	*She holds your Isis?*
Janet	She holds my necklace from Isis, and she goes toward the east.
Raleigh	*She goes toward the east?*
Janet	She will return from the east, and she will give it back.
Raleigh	*So she has it right now?*
Janet	She guards it with me; she gives me power. She holds my necklace close to her heart.
Raleigh	*So you don't keep the necklace with you?*
Janet	Not when they bury me. She takes it. She takes it for my soul. She will come again, and we will ride on the horse.
Raleigh	*Alright, let's back up a moment.*
Janet	Alright.
Raleigh	*Who was the actual woman? What did she go by for a name?*
Janet	No.
Raleigh	*Say it again, please.*

Janet	No! You will look for her. [Sob.]
Raleigh	*No, I won't look for her. I'm sorry, I won't ask that again.*
Janet	[Whisper.] She holds my power. She protects me. [Sob.]
Raleigh	*Let's talk about your childhood. Let's go to pleasant times when you were young. What did you like to do? Other than ride your horse. What games did you like to do?*
Janet	Games?
Raleigh	*Fun things to do.*
Janet	I like the water.
Raleigh	*Could you swim?*
Janet	Yeah.
Raleigh	*Where did you swim?*
Janet	In the bath house. The women stayed in the bath house.
Raleigh	*The women stayed in the bath house?*
Janet	Yeah, they were special women.
Raleigh	*What was special about them?*
Janet	They were virgins. I could stay in there. The guards would let me come and go because I'm a princess. A princess can go anywhere.
Raleigh	*Did they protect you all the time, or were there guards with you always?*
Janet	Not in the bath house!
Raleigh	*How about everywhere else?*
Janet	Not in the bedroom. My Lady lives in the bedroom.
Raleigh	*Okay. The same lady that took you to the stars?*
Janet	Yes, I play.
Raleigh	*You play. Did you have friends?*
Janet	Sometimes I play with the other children.

Raleigh	*Did you have brothers or sisters?*
Janet	I don't know them.
Raleigh	*You don't know them? Does that mean you did or didn't?*
Janet	I don't know.
Raleigh	*All you know is you?*
Janet	Yes.
Raleigh	*Did you ever see your mother?*
Janet	The Goddess?
Raleigh	*Yes, the Goddess. But did you ever see her?*
Janet	Yeah.
Raleigh	*[At this point I had some Egyptian art that I brought out. There were several characters in the picture of men and women.] Do you see her in this picture?*
Janet	Oh, yes. [She points to her mother, Isis, in the picture correctly.] She's so beautiful.
Raleigh	*[I point to the picture of Osiris, their version of Jesus.] Is this your father?*
Janet	That's God!
Raleigh	*That is God, so that is not your father?*
Janet	He will let my spirit go, and I will avenge those who murdered my father.
Raleigh	*Is … any of the people in this painting your father?*
Janet	No.
Raleigh	*Okay, now open your eyes and look at me. I look different than your people, don't I?*
Janet	Yes.
Raleigh	*Is there anything you would like to say?*
Janet	Everything looks different.
Raleigh	*That's the way it is. Time has passed, thousands of years have gone by since your time. You are from a different part of the world.*

Janet	Your jewelry [pointing to my painting] — I know him, I know him! [Now pointing at my earphones around my neck.] I don't know him.
Raleigh	*Oh! I understand. This isn't jewelry. Right now I'm listening to your voice, and I have a device that will record your voice. So some other day when I'm not talking to you, and I want to listen to what you have told me, I can push a button so I can hear your voice all over again. Okay, now let's get back to where we were. Were the guards nice to you?*
Janet	They carry me when I want them to.
Raleigh	*Oh, so they carry you when you want them to.*
Janet	Yes, but I'm not supposed to let them do it much, because it doesn't look very lady-like.
Raleigh	*Did they like doing that?*
Janet	Carrying me?
Raleigh	*Yes.*
Janet	Yes, at least they seemed to.
Raleigh	*So they liked you?*
Janet	Yes, I always gave them a good laugh because I'm silly.
Raleigh	*What makes them laugh?*
Janet	There are two things: pretend that I can't walk — you know, like when they have drunk too much of the wine — and the way they do all of that dumb stuff. Ha-ha-ha-ha.
Raleigh	*So you act that way?*
Janet	Oh yeah, but I don't make that stuff come out … yuck … ooooh no.
Raleigh	*And that makes them laugh?*
Janet	Yeah.
Raleigh	*Is it because it's the Princess doing this?*

Janet	Yeah.
Raleigh	*How old are you when you are doing this?*
Janet	Oh, five.
Raleigh	*Do the guards have a special name they call you?*
Janet	Yeah, they just call me Princess or Butterfly. But I don't know why Butterfly. I don't know what a butterfly is. They say you have wings and I can fly. But I don't have wings, I have snakes. But don't tell anyone.
Raleigh	*Okay. Did your dad know you had the snakes?*
Janet	My dad is very proud that I wear the snakes.
Raleigh	*Okay, now without putting your own feelings into it, we are now going to the time of your death. You were, as stated earlier, approximately 18, correct?*
Janet	Yes.
Raleigh	*Did you ever see any men that you liked?*
Janet	They were not for me to ....
Raleigh	*Okay, if they would have been, did you see some you were attracted to?*
Janet	A child king.
Raleigh	*He was pretty special?*
Janet	He looked like my father.
Raleigh	*Where did you see him at?*
Janet	When his father died.
Raleigh	*How old was this child king?*
Janet	I don't know. He was a little boy.
Raleigh	*How old were you at the time?*
Janet	I was seven.
Raleigh	*And he was a child. How old?*
Janet	Nine.
Raleigh	*You thought he was pretty handsome?*
Janet	Oh, yes, he was gorgeous.

Raleigh	*Did you see him become King, or was he already King?*
Janet	He just became King.
Raleigh	*How far from your home was this?*
Janet	It was on the Nile.
Raleigh	*Were you going with the current or against the current?*
Janet	It's hot and I have to stay covered.
Raleigh	*Let's put it this way, when you were traveling on the water, were you just floating or was it hard work?*
Janet	I didn't have to do anything.
Raleigh	*Okay, how about the men that were doing the work? Were they having to work hard?*
Janet	I don't think so. They don't smell.
Raleigh	*Are you that close that you could tell?*
Janet	Yuck!
Raleigh	*Ha-ha-ha. I take it you are. Where were you when this hit you?*
Janet	What?
Raleigh	*The smell.*
Janet	It was right there! [Pointing to an armpit.]
Raleigh	*Oh! You smelled one, okay.*
Janet	Yuck, cough, gag!
Raleigh	*When you were on the ship, you actually did that?*
Janet	You asked if they had worked hard. How do you know if they worked hard if they don't smell?
Raleigh	*And that was the test?*
Janet	They stinks!
Raleigh	*They stinks?*
Janet	He does, and I'm not smelling anymore! Yuck!
Raleigh	*What color are these men?*
Janet	They are darker than the sand.
Raleigh	*Are you darker than them?*
Janet	No.

Raleigh	*Are these soldiers?*
Janet	Yeah, they go everywhere I travel.
Raleigh	*Are the ones guiding the boat soldiers as well?*
Janet	We have a different class of people.
Raleigh	*Okay, go on.*
Janet	There are some that will give us food because we give them land and protect them. So they do special favors for us.
Raleigh	*So taking you on this boat is one of them?*
Janet	Well, the boat belongs to my dad; but they will take us, and they will do the work. That's their special favor. It's just like when I get old they will build my pyramid. They will do special things because we take care of them.
Raleigh	*Did you actually watch them build it?*
Janet	I can watch if I want, when I get older.
Raleigh	*Did you?*
Janet	Yes.
Raleigh	*How did they do it?*
Janet	They had logs. They took ropes, they push it, then they stack. The men have special things they put on their feet, and they can climb right up the side. They go up just like a spider.
Raleigh	*Okay, how large is this pyramid?*
Janet	From my rock to my star rock?
Raleigh	*What do you call the star rock?*
Janet	My point. They have told me there are 21.
Raleigh	*Twenty-one stones going up?*
Janet	They miscounted, you know that, don't you?
Raleigh	*Who did?*
Janet	When they stopped.
Raleigh	*What should it have been?*

Janet	Nineteen.
Raleigh	*So, what did they do?*
Janet	They had to make that point.
Raleigh	*Was there a reason for the 19?*
Janet	I died.
Raleigh	*A stone for each year you were alive?*
Janet	Yes. They had 21. They had to make 19 the point.
Raleigh	*They killed your father, and they killed you. But they still did this work for your pyramid?*
Janet	Yes, they fear … they fear … they fear Isis.
Raleigh	*So they did this ceremony out of fear?*
Janet	My Lady marked my tomb.
Raleigh	*In what way?*
Janet	If they desecrate me — if they don't bury me with my honors — my mother, Isis, will wipe them out.
Raleigh	*Oh! And that was the mark on the tomb?*
Janet	That's my mark.
Raleigh	*Is this something they would know, once they see it?*
Janet	When they see the mark of Isis, then they will know.
Raleigh	*So, it's the mark of Isis that they will fear?*
Janet	A special mark.
Raleigh	*Let me ask you this … in the many thousands of years since your time, many tombs have been found. Many have been plundered. Many have been put into museums ….*
Janet	Tutankhamen, they awakened him.
Raleigh	*They woke him?*
Janet	They awoke his flesh. He told me in the stars.
Raleigh	*They awoke his flesh?*
Janet	He can see … he can see, and they awoke his flesh ….
Raleigh	*Yes?*

Janet	And they dug.
Raleigh	*They dug.*
Janet	He said, "When they find me, they will awaken my flesh."
Raleigh	*How about you?*
Janet	When they find me, they will dig and they will awaken my flesh. They will open my sarcophagus, but they won't find my necklace.
Raleigh	*They will find your body but not your necklace?*
Janet	They will find my flesh but not my soul.
Raleigh	*I understand, so your flesh hasn't been found yet?*
Janet	No.
Raleigh	*A question was just asked by my wife. What you are saying is your soul is with your necklace?*
Janet	It is the mark of Isis and the psychic of the Egyptian.
Raleigh	*So the answer to the question is yes?*
Janet	What is the question?
Raleigh	*That the necklace holds your soul.*
Janet	It holds my power to come between this earth and the other.
Raleigh	*Okay, this is allowing you to come from your side to my side, to talk to me.*
Janet	You asked me to come, did you not?
Raleigh	*Yes, I did.*
Janet	Okay.
Raleigh	*And the necklace allows you to do that.*
Janet	I come when there is pain. I have the power to heal.
Raleigh	*Okay, let's go to the time which you actually passed on.*
Janet	They stabbed me with the knife!
Raleigh	*We're going to what happened next.*

Janet	I'm at the door, and there's the guard outside.
Raleigh	*Didn't he see the man come in?*
Janet	But he's not my father's guard. He is with the man who calls my father "Brother." He enters my room with a mask over his face.
Raleigh	*What type of a mask is it?*
Janet	It's dark, like a warrior wears.
Raleigh	*So he came in and stabbed you. Did he say anything when he did?*
Janet	To forgive him.
Raleigh	*To forgive him?*
Janet	Yes. He's a greedy man; he wants everything. Then, the demon inside of him wants it … but I don't know the demon inside of him. And the knife is the knife used in rituals!
Raleigh	*The knife is used in rituals?*
Janet	Yes, and he will pay dearly for stabbing me with that, for I have done no wrong!
Raleigh	*He will pay dearly for stabbing you with the knife?*
Janet	He will have a very painful death, and he will not go to heaven! He will not go! He will burn!
Raleigh	*Did you die immediately?*
Janet	No, I make a sound: keeeee … my lungs … they won't go up; they won't go down!
Raleigh	*So you couldn't talk?*
Janet	No!
Raleigh	*I don't want you to feel the pain. I only want you to tell me what is happening, okay?*
Janet	Okay.
Raleigh	*Now, he said, "Forgive me." Did you pull the mask off of him?*
Janet	I make him take it off.

Raleigh	*Oh! You did?*
Janet	I am the Princess, the daughter of Isis, the Goddess. Why should he not show me his face if he asks me for forgiveness? How can I forgive if I don't know who killed me?
Raleigh	*Did you forgive him?*
Janet	No!
Raleigh	*No, did you tell him no?*
Janet	I told him no! I did not know the demon of which he speaks of, only that he is selfish and fat! He cares not of anyone else! He just does not know how to treat his people! He takes their food! He takes everything! His special people, he beats them! He's not good to his special people!
Raleigh	*So he is a protector over people as well?*
Janet	Oh yes, but he's no good.
Raleigh	*So he's like a king?*
Janet	But he wants both kingdoms.
Raleigh	*Oh, so he was a king somewhere else?*
Janet	Oh yes, and he is not the friend of Tutankhamen either. He is not a friend of a child who is king. He is not a friend to anyone!
Raleigh	*Now we go to where you have already died. What happened next?*
Janet	They take this body. They lay it on a table. I'm not in the body.
Raleigh	*Are you in the room with your body?*
Janet	Yes, it's so exciting!
Raleigh	*Why is that?*
Janet	I have never gotten to see this when I was little.
Raleigh	*But now it is being done to you.*

Janet	It is being done to my body, not to me. I am not in my body.
Raleigh	*I understand. So, what are they doing?*
Janet	They take some long things and put them in there [indicating nose], and they turn them and turn them. Then they take them back out. They are working very quickly. They have seven days.
Raleigh	*Why seven days? This would be a very short time.*
Janet	They are scared.
Raleigh	*Oh, so they want to do this fast?*
Janet	They don't do all of me. They put my insides in little jars, and they don't put me back together either.
Raleigh	*So this was done very quickly?*
Janet	They fear Isis. They see the mark. It's branded on my cheek.
Raleigh	*Was this always on your cheek?*
Janet	All I can remember is always, since I was a little girl.
Raleigh	*So, you always remember having it?*
Janet	The mark of Isis, the mark of the Psychic Child on my butt.
Raleigh	*On your butt? Okay, so no one saw it.*
Janet	That is why I'm so special. That is why I have the two snakes. The mark of the psychic allows me to come from my world to you.
Raleigh	*So they prepared your body and did a rush job on it?*
Janet	They didn't really do very good, but they are scared.
Raleigh	*What do they talk about when they do this?*
Janet	They pray. They pray for the walls to not fall upon them. They pray for Isis to forgive them. They pray for the demon in my uncle. THEY PRAY!

Raleigh	*So they are pretty scared.*
Janet	They shake. I feel their hands — they shake on my body — they shake like shaking me.
Raleigh	*Okay, they're that scared?*
Janet	They want me out of there. They wrap me quick. They don't put me all back together.
Raleigh	*Okay, they don't put you all back together, but they do take you to your pyramid?*
Janet	They have to. They cannot have me not buried properly.
Raleigh	*Did they bury you inside your pyramid?*
Janet	Yes.
Raleigh	*Were procedures done differently because you were killed, rather than die naturally?*
Janet	My uncle wants people to think I was killed by my father. He calls him a murderer that ran away.
Raleigh	*Your father was killed before you?*
Janet	Same day.
Raleigh	*But not at the same time?*
Janet	My father was killed in the morning, and I was killed in the late evening.
Raleigh	*Did you know of your father's death?*
Janet	I felt it. [Sob, sob.] I felt sad for my father's flesh. He was good to his people.
Raleigh	*Knowing your father went before you, did he wait for you? On the other side?*
Janet	Of course! I'm his Princess! He waits for me to come, back at the light.
Raleigh	*So he is still waiting at the light?*
Janet	He knew when I came down.
Raleigh	*Can you see him right now?*
Janet	He watches me.

Raleigh	*Is he pleased by all this?*
Janet	I'm not sure that he understands, but he knows I have to travel back and forth.
Raleigh	*So he's not bothered by me?*
Janet	Oh, no. He told me I can speak.
Raleigh	*Over time, why has your tomb not been found? What has happened to your pyramid?*
Janet	It is guarded by ancient secrets more powerful than Tutankhamen.
Raleigh	*I'm not trying to find it, but did something happen to it?*
Janet	Oh, did the earth shake it?
Raleigh	*Yes.*
Janet	No, the earth didn't shake it, and the water didn't wash it away.
Raleigh	*So it is still standing today?*
Janet	Oh, yes.
Raleigh	*So, if it still stands today, surely someone has entered it.*
Janet	They have not come out. One man … one man — he wears a turban around his head — he scratches on the walls.
Raleigh	*But they haven't entered your tomb yet?*
Janet	No, but he makes it ugly. It is still mine!
Raleigh	*What will you think when someone enters it?*
Janet	Will they have a good heart, like my father, or mean like my uncle?
Raleigh	*I can't answer that.*
Janet	If they are good to my father's people, I would be good to them. Forgive me, but if they are mean like my father's brother, I would make them pay the curse!

Raleigh   *Let me ask you this: if I was the one who found your tomb, what would you do?*

Janet   My father said I can talk to you. My father knows man. You could go.

Raleigh   *Would it surprise you that I did see the treasures of Tutankhamen? Yet tears came to my eyes, and I had to leave the room.*

Janet   It's because you have a heart. Why did you cry?

Raleigh   *It was because that was his and nobody was to see. I felt ... as beautiful and precious as the things that he had — which were more beautiful than anything I had ever seen — these things were his alone and were not to be viewed on display. It upset me greatly. [Janet turns her head.] What are you looking at?*

Janet   My father.

Raleigh   *What's he saying?*

Janet   He said you cry from your soul. You did not steal from the Child King!

Raleigh   *No, I did not.*

Janet   You did not! You are not cursed from the Child King! They killed the Child King, too!

Raleigh   *They killed the Child King, too?*

Janet   Yeah.

Raleigh   *Same type of reason? Greed?*

Janet   Yeah, he told me they crushed his skull.

Raleigh   *They crushed his skull?*

Janet   Yeah.

Raleigh   *Was it the same men?*

Janet   You mean my uncle?

Raleigh   *Yes.*

Janet   He did not do it! He did not do it! He knew those who did do it!

Raleigh	*He did know those who did do it?*
Janet	Yes, they are all greedy.
Raleigh	*They are all greedy, okay. Let's go on. When you left the funeral parlor and they took you to your pyramid, what did you see next?*
Janet	I am following my body to my resting place. It was filled with food and wine and my servants.
Raleigh	*You have servants?*
Janet	You have to have them — they go with you — and my soldier … one soldier … one soldier.
Raleigh	*One soldier?*
Janet	Yes, one soldier, and he will guard my entrance.
Raleigh	*He guards the entrance?*
Janet	Yes, but this time he guards from the inside, and it is … it is an honor to be chosen.
Raleigh	*It's an honor to be chosen? Does that go for the servants as well?*
Janet	The servants are chosen by your mother. And when you grow, your servants grow with you; and they know what you need, what you like. They know you. They are like your mother.
Raleigh	*So they are with you all the way along?*
Janet	Yeah.
Raleigh	*If you go, they go?*
Janet	They will be there to feed my soul when it is hungry.
Raleigh	*Alright, now everyone has left. Where do you go from there?*
Janet	Out the top.
Raleigh	*Out the top?*
Janet	Yes.
Raleigh	*Then to where?*
Janet	To the stars. There is a light.

Raleigh	*There's a light? What about the light you see?*
Janet	It's on the bottom of the little cup.
Raleigh	*The bottom of the little cup?*
Janet	[Softly.] Yeah ....
Raleigh	*And that's where you go?*
Janet	The light is so bright and warm.
Raleigh	*What are you told when you get there?*
Janet	What am I told?
Raleigh	*Yes. Did you see anyone ... when you get there?*
Janet	[Softly.] I have to be judged. [Loudly.] I don't fear that!
Raleigh	*Okay, you don't fear that. Who do you see when you are being judged?*
Janet	Those that have been passed before me.
Raleigh	*What do they say about you?*
Janet	They weighed my heart. They weighed my spirit. They weighed my soul.
Raleigh	*And is it good?*
Janet	Yes, they know me. I never had to say. They knew without me saying. They know when you lie, too. It's not good to lie to them. [Big smile.]
Raleigh	*Ha-ha. So you didn't lie to them.*
Janet	I didn't have to lie. But the man before me, he lied.
Raleigh	*He did?*
Janet	Yes, and his heart was gone. He made it to the other side, but he didn't make it past the second skill.
Raleigh	*There are two?*
Janet	Yeah. [Janet points in different directions.] You go here, and they read your heart and soul. You go here, and they say yes or no. When he went here, he lied and they knew. So when he went here, he had to go.

Raleigh *So … went and saw God then?*

Janet You call Him God.

Raleigh *Yes, you went and saw the One we call God.*

Janet And my mother and father.

Raleigh *When you met God, what was said to you?*

Janet I can tell you I am welcome there.

Raleigh *That is what He is telling you?*

Janet That is all I can tell you. I am welcome there. Do you understand?

Raleigh *Yes, you are in contact with them right now, aren't you?*

Janet You mean do I hear them?

Raleigh *Yes.*

Janet Yes! I am there now!

Raleigh *Will you help me, someday, look for children who are gone?*

Janet There is no vengeance in this world. I feel the pain of the child in this world.

Raleigh *My question is … will you help me find the lost?*

Janet Yes.

EPISODE 6

◆ Trees, Water, Mountains ◆

RECENTLY IN DALLAS, I was invited for supper at the home of a co-worker and his family from the Netherlands. Ton and Marie have two very cute kids who remind me a great deal of my own grandchildren. I originally went over to help Marie quit smoking because Ton had seen me hypnotize someone during a trip to Nebraska. Marie, however, was very skeptical.

Since Marie is Dutch, there was a small language problem from time to time even though she speaks very good English. When she entered the past life, however, there was no such problem. What I really enjoy about a session like this is the lack of knowledge of past-life regression. Before I put Marie to sleep, I asked if she could live in any time period what it would be. She said she feels strongly about the Native American Indians and, in fact, she collects their art.

This episode shows that God wants us to be tolerant of one another and to correct our mistakes.

Raleigh	*We are now going to another time, another place, a place you know nothing of. What do you see?*
Marie	Trees. Water. Mountains.
Raleigh	*Okay, slow down. You are seeing trees and water?*
Marie	And mountains.
Raleigh	*Okay, what about the mountains? Is it summer time, winter time, what?*
Marie	Winter, spring. Half snow, half green.

Raleigh	*Where are you?*
Marie	I'm sitting near the water.
Raleigh	*Is there anyone with you?*
Marie	No.
Raleigh	*How old are you?*
Marie	Twenty-five.
Raleigh	*What do people call you when they call you by name?*
Marie	Mambella.
Raleigh	*Mambella?*
Marie	Mambella, uh-huh, like the wind.
Raleigh	*Describe yourself. What do you look like?*
Marie	Long hair.
Raleigh	*Long hair, okay. What color is it?*
Marie	Black.
Raleigh	*Okay, how are you dressed?*
Marie	Brown dress.
Raleigh	*A brown dress? What is it made from?*
Marie	From buffalo.
Raleigh	*From buffalo?*
Marie	I'm washing.
Raleigh	*Washing what?*
Marie	Pans.
Raleigh	*Pants?*
Marie	Like a cooking pan.
Raleigh	*Are you married?*
Marie	No.
Raleigh	*Are you in what would be called the United States?*
Marie	I'm in my land.
Raleigh	*Okay, you are in your land.*
Marie	I don't know this United States. I don't think so. It's cold.

Raleigh	*Are there a lot of members of the tribe where you are from?*
Marie	Yes.
Raleigh	*Do you have brothers and sisters?*
Marie	One brother.
Raleigh	*One brother?*
Marie	Yeah.
Raleigh	*Older or younger than you?*
Marie	Older, he's married.
Raleigh	*What is your brother's name?*
Marie	Tombel.
Raleigh	*Say it again, please.*
Marie	Tombel.
Raleigh	*Are you nervous about talking to me?*
Marie	Umm ....
Raleigh	*Does this bother you?*
Marie	Maybe a little bit.
Raleigh	*A little bit, okay. You're not afraid though?*
Marie	Umm, no.
Raleigh	*You know I'm not going to hurt you, correct?*
Marie	Umm, I don't know.
Raleigh	*Well, I'm not. We're just talking. Okay?*
Marie	Umm ....
Raleigh	*What year is it right now?*
Marie	I don't know ... wait ... 1800, I think.
Raleigh	*What makes you think that?*
Marie	I hear something like that.
Raleigh	*Who said it?*
Marie	My brother.
Raleigh	*What brought the conversation up about it being 1800?*
Marie	He came back from the other people.

Raleigh	*What other people?*
Marie	The ones living across the river. Bad people.
Raleigh	*Bad people?*
Marie	Yes, bad people.
Raleigh	*What is bad about them?*
Marie	DEATH! Other stuff!
Raleigh	*What do you mean?*
Marie	They kill people.
Raleigh	*What color are these people?*
Marie	Lighter than me, white.
Raleigh	*They are white?*
Marie	Yes, white.
Raleigh	*Are you afraid of these people?*
Marie	Yes.
Raleigh	*Have you ever talked to them?*
Marie	Noooo! Noooo! [Very afraid.]
Raleigh	*No?*
Marie	No, you are the first one!
Raleigh	*How do you know that I am white?*
Marie	I see you. [Eyes are shut.]
Raleigh	*You can see me?*
Marie	I see you.
Raleigh	*But you don't feel bad talking to me, though.*
Marie	No, it's okay. I'm afraid.
Raleigh	*You're afraid?*
Marie	Yes.
Raleigh	*Of me?*
Marie	Not of people like you, I heard noises.
Raleigh	*You heard noises?*
Marie	… Yes …. [Said very cautiously.]
Raleigh	*You are by the water. Is that right?*
Marie	Yes.

Raleigh	*Alright, we want to slow down here for a moment. Okay?*
Marie	Yes.
Raleigh	*I am going to tell you something, and I want you to try to understand. Okay?*
Marie	Umm hmm.
Raleigh	*At this time, these things have already happened. Alright? At this time it will be very difficult for you to understand, but we will just go slowly. Okay?*
Marie	Umm hmm.
Raleigh	*Just trust me when I tell you that. I will not lie to you. I don't know what is about to happen, all I can tell you is that it has already happened. Alright?*
Marie	Umm.
Raleigh	*Will you believe me about this?*
Marie	Yes.
Raleigh	*You heard noises, correct?*
Marie	Yes.
Raleigh	*What were the noises?*
Marie	In the woods I hear something … a stick.
Raleigh	*A stick? Like a stick breaking?*
Marie	Yes.
Raleigh	*Alright, let's stop here for a moment. You said you are 25. Is that right?*
Marie	Yes.
Raleigh	*I want you to tell me, did you see age 26?*
Marie	I'm married!
Raleigh	*You're married?*
Marie	Umm, yes, 26.
Raleigh	*Okay then, let's go back to when you were 25. We know nothing happened to you.*
Marie	No.
Raleigh	*What did the noise turn out to be?*

Marie	A deer.
Raleigh	*Ha-ha, a deer.*
Marie	It was going to get some water.
Raleigh	*It scared you?*
Marie	Yeah.
Raleigh	*What did you think it was?*
Marie	Your people!
Raleigh	*My people?*
Marie	I can't talk that long to you.
Raleigh	*Why?*
Marie	I have to get back to my people. I can't be seen with you.
Raleigh	*Okay, let's now go to age 26. You were telling me you are married. Is that right?*
Marie	Yes.
Raleigh	*Who did you marry?*
Marie	My husband.
Raleigh	*Ha-ha, okay. What was his name?*
Marie	I don't know if I can tell you that.
Raleigh	*Why is that?*
Marie	Your people are looking for him.
Raleigh	*My people are looking for him?*
Marie	Yes.
Raleigh	*Why?*
Marie	He killed somebody.
Raleigh	*He killed somebody? Did he really do it?*
Marie	Umm, yes. [Sigh.] He was taking food.
Raleigh	*He was taking food?*
Marie	Yeah.
Raleigh	*Is that a reason to kill somebody?*
Marie	I don't know. He was taking food.
Raleigh	*Were your people hungry?*

Marie	They had enough.
Raleigh	*They had enough, but he was still taking food?*
Marie	The white man was taking the food.
Raleigh	*Oh! The white man was taking the food.*
Marie	Yeah. He is hungry. He is taking food.
Raleigh	*Okay.*
Marie	He deserved it. Don't take food from us!
Raleigh	*You knew your husband had killed someone?*
Marie	Yeah, oh yeah. [Very nervous.] I was there.
Raleigh	*YOU WERE THERE?*
Marie	Yes.
Raleigh	*What did you think about that?*
Marie	He deserved it. Don't take our food!
Raleigh	*You told him not to take your food?*
Marie	Yeah.
Raleigh	*Is that when the problem started?*
Marie	Yeah.
Raleigh	*Okay, let me clarify something here. You keep saying it's my people.*
Marie	Umm hmm, yes.
Raleigh	*These were my ancestors, okay? They are not my people of today. Things have changed over time. All I am asking is for you to tell us your story, okay?*
Marie	Yes.
Raleigh	*Everything you are telling me has already happened, okay?*
Marie	Hmm?
Raleigh	*Remember when you were telling me about being beside the lake?*
Marie	Yes.
Raleigh	*Now you are 26.*
Marie	Yes.

Raleigh	*Do you now understand things have already happened? It feels like it was just yesterday, doesn't it?*
Marie	Yes!
Raleigh	*The more we talk, the more you will understand. Okay?*
Marie	Yes.
Raleigh	*You don't have to worry about your people seeing me because they can't see me.*
Marie	Okay.
Raleigh	*As far as your husband is concerned … it was a very, very long time ago … for me.*
Marie	Okay.
Raleigh	*Did anyone ever find your husband?*
Marie	He's fine. He's with me.
Raleigh	*So you left with him?*
Marie	Yes. He's with me, with my paw paw.
Raleigh	*Are you saying your child?*
Marie	No, my paw paw.
Raleigh	*Your dad?*
Marie	Yes, my paw paw.
Raleigh	*Did you all leave together?*
Marie	We went back to the town, my village. My husband is in the woods.
Raleigh	*He's in the woods?*
Marie	Yes. He has his hair.
Raleigh	*He has whose hair?*
Marie	The white man.
Raleigh	*You have the white man's hair?*
Marie	Yeah. [Almost a small laugh.]
Raleigh	*Oh! So when he killed him, he took the hair?*
Marie	Yeah.
Raleigh	*Why?*

Marie	So they will leave us alone. You stay off my land, and I will stay off your land!
Raleigh	*Did you see age 30?*
Marie	No.
Raleigh	*Did you see age 28?*
Marie	A baby.
Raleigh	*A baby?*
Marie	Yes, laying in my hands.
Raleigh	*There is a baby laying in your hands? Is it your baby?*
Marie	Yes.
Raleigh	*Same husband?*
Marie	Yes.
Raleigh	*So nobody ever killed him?*
Marie	No, he's gone away to get food … something.
Raleigh	*Is your baby well?*
Marie	Yes, it's crying.
Raleigh	*Are you well?*
Marie	Yes.
Raleigh	*Is your father still alive?*
Marie	No, he's been killed. The white people … they killed my whole village.
Raleigh	*Why did they kill your village?*
Marie	Because we killed the white man.
Raleigh	*The one your husband took the scalp from?*
Marie	Yes, they took revenge. They killed my father.
Raleigh	*Let me ask you this … killing is wrong no matter how it's done ….*
Marie	No! You take our food, you must be killed!
Raleigh	*Is that your law? So if one of your people took food from one of your people, you would have to kill them?*

Marie	They would be killed. They would be a traitor. The white people said if we would give them food, they would give us your weapons to help do the hunting.
Raleigh	*A gun?*
Marie	Yes, a gun, but they didn't do it.
Raleigh	*So they didn't do it?*
Marie	No, they promised.
Raleigh	*So this is why the man was killed?*
Marie	Yes. He was just taking our food.
Raleigh	*But not giving anything? Okay, and you were promised guns?*
Marie	Yes.
Raleigh	*Were the white people hungry?*
Marie	They didn't know how to hunt.
Raleigh	*Were they like farmers?*
Marie	No.
Raleigh	*Where did they come from?*
Marie	I don't know. They came with guns, wagons, and horses.
Raleigh	*What did your people think the very first time you saw them?*
Marie	We attacked them.
Raleigh	*You attacked them! So the very first time you saw these people you attacked them?*
Marie	Yes. They had great guns. We lost a lot of people.
Raleigh	*Okay, you didn't even get a chance to talk to these people. You just attacked them.*
Marie	We were watching what they were doing. They were making houses on our land.
Raleigh	*Did your people ever tell them, "We don't want you to be here"?*
Marie	No.

Raleigh	*You just attacked?*
Marie	Yes.
Raleigh	*At age 28 you had a baby in your arms, but you never saw age 30. Is that right?*
Marie	No.
Raleigh	*Did you see age 29?*
Marie	No.
Raleigh	*Are you beginning to understand that these things have already happened?*
Marie	Yes.
Raleigh	*Are you still afraid of me?*
Marie	No, not much.
Raleigh	*Somewhere between age 28 and age 29 something happened to you, didn't it?*
Marie	Yes.
Raleigh	*Just tell me what happened.*
Marie	I went down to the river to get some water. I heard some men talking. I was hiding.
Raleigh	*Where is the baby?*
Marie	He's dead.
Raleigh	*What happened to your baby?*
Marie	Cold winter. It was too cold for him.
Raleigh	*The winter was too cold and the baby died?*
Marie	Yes.
Raleigh	*Did your husband come back?*
Marie	Yes.
Raleigh	*What did he say about the child dying?*
Marie	It was my fault.
Raleigh	*Was he there when it happened?*
Marie	No, he was hunting. He was gone.
Raleigh	*Did you have food during that time?*
Marie	Not much, only some fish. It's cold.

Raleigh	*Were there other men around who could help you?*
Marie	The men are all gone. They are all hunting. Only three men ... my paw paw ... my father.
Raleigh	*Were there other women in the area to help you?*
Marie	No.
Raleigh	*Why?*
Marie	They didn't have food either. It's cold, very cold. Children die, eight children.
Raleigh	*Okay, let's go back to the river. You were hiding. You heard men talking.*
Marie	Yes. Three of them. They betrayed us.
Raleigh	*Who betrayed you?*
Marie	Another white man who came to our village asking for food. He came earlier asking for food. We gave it to him. We don't have that much.
Raleigh	*Okay.*
Marie	And also their people died from the cold winter.
Raleigh	*Okay.*
Marie	What I tried to understand was that we were told it was our fault the white people, children died.
Raleigh	*It was your fault?*
Marie	Yes, it was our fault.
Raleigh	*Why?*
Marie	Because we didn't give them food and because we burned the land, our land.
Raleigh	*Wait a minute! You burned the land?*
Marie	Yes, they were making things in our land so we burned it.
Raleigh	*Is that why there was a food shortage?*
Marie	Yes.

Raleigh	*Let me stop so I can write all this down, but I have a question about that. Let me put it this way … your people have lived off the land for a long time, correct?*
Marie	Yes.
Raleigh	*Now people come in. Have your people survived off the land?*
Marie	Yes.
Raleigh	*They had to have a respect for the land, correct?*
Marie	Yes.
Raleigh	*Now don't get me wrong on this, but wasn't that kind of stupid to burn the land knowing you wouldn't have anything to eat?*
Marie	It was our land. They took it away from us.
Raleigh	*I understand that.*
Marie	We were mad. We want it back.
Raleigh	*If you burned it, you wouldn't have anything either. Nobody would have anything.*
Marie	They didn't give us nothing … building something. Food, it went to the next year. So we burned it down.
Raleigh	*Okay, they were supposed to give you something.*
Marie	We gave them food in the beginning, and they will give us guns. That never happened. Then they start building some food on the land. It was our land, we got nothing from them.
Raleigh	*So let's put it this way. You would rather burn the land, starve to death, starve your children to death, rather than give them the land?*
Marie	Yes, it's our land.
Raleigh	*But you would have no food.*
Marie	We have food. The hunting of the deer.
Raleigh	*Was it enough to keep the people alive?*

Marie	No, not my baby.
Raleigh	*So, it wasn't a very wise decision to burn the land, was it?*
Marie	No.
Raleigh	*Whose idea was it to burn the land?*
Marie	Paw Paw.
Raleigh	*Your father's idea? I thought he was already dead?*
Marie	No, not at that time. He said we would have to burn the land. We have more than one daddy, I don't know how to say … like the chief.
Raleigh	*Yes.*
Marie	They call him always Daddy.
Raleigh	*So this was not your actual father?*
Marie	No.
Raleigh	*But they called them Fathers?*
Marie	Yes. He was the chief. They call him Chief.
Raleigh	*Being a woman, did they ask for your opinion?*
Marie	Nooo!
Raleigh	*If you would have had an opinion, what would it have been? Would you have thought this isn't a very good idea?*
Marie	No, I want revenge.
Raleigh	*You want revenge?*
Marie	They killed my baby. My baby starved to death. They didn't give me nothing.
Raleigh	*Let's go once more along the water.*
Marie	Okay.
Raleigh	*You said you were betrayed by an individual you gave food to.*
Marie	Yes.
Raleigh	*And when you say betrayed, what do you mean by that?*

Marie	I was helping him, to give him food from us. I was helping him because he had a wife and a baby. He was good. He gave me some deer when he was hunting on the deer and the rabbit. One time he gave me two rabbits. I have some meat, some food. But he betrayed us. He was talking to another man.
Raleigh	*Okay.*
Marie	They said, "All the men have gone hunting." I know a little bit of their language now.
Raleigh	*As I am talking to you now, are you hearing it in your language?*
Marie	Yes.
Raleigh	*And when you are speaking to me?*
Marie	It is my language.
Raleigh	*Is what you are saying what you are hearing?*
Marie	It sounds different.
Raleigh	*Do you know that I am white?*
Marie	Yes.
Raleigh	*What were these men planning?*
Marie	I hear them talking about revenge for when we tried to take back the land.
Raleigh	*In what way?*
Marie	They want to kill all the wives and their children. I said, "No!" I run back.
Raleigh	*Did anyone hear you?*
Marie	No, I'm to the village.
Raleigh	*When you went back, what did you tell them?*
Marie	"We must go to the woods! Go to the woods! They're coming!"
Raleigh	*Did they?*
Marie	Paw Paw said, "No, don't go. Don't run away. We will fight."

Raleigh	*Was there a fight?*
Marie	Yes … a lot of blood.
Raleigh	*A lot of blood. Did you get killed here?*
Marie	Yes.
Raleigh	*What happened to you?*
Marie	I see a man riding on his horse. I'm trying to get him.
Raleigh	*You're trying to get him?*
Marie	Yes [softly], but he shot me. I'm bleeding.
Raleigh	*How were you trying to get him?*
Marie	I was trying to get his horse. Try to make it fall down.
Raleigh	*Where did he shoot you?*
Marie	Umm … in my stomach … bleeding.
Raleigh	*Did you die?*
Marie	Yes.
Raleigh	*What happened after you died? What happened next?*
Marie	I see myself dying away. I go to the clouds. I see myself lying in the grass.
Raleigh	*You looked back?*
Marie	Yes.
Raleigh	*Let me ask you this. In your culture, where did you go after you died?*
Marie	You go further. Your soul goes with the wind.
Raleigh	*Your soul goes with the wind?*
Marie	Yes.
Raleigh	*Where would it end up?*
Marie	To an animal.
Raleigh	*To an animal?*
Marie	Yes, like a bird high above the ground.
Raleigh	*That's what you were told?*
Marie	Yes.
Raleigh	*Did you have a belief in a god?*

Marie   You believe in heaven and sky.

Raleigh   *Was that part of it?*

Marie   When the people are mad, the thunder and the light will take you off.

Raleigh   *So you feel it was beings throwing the thunder and lightning like a god?*

Marie   This is why they are mad and had no food for us. We didn't trust our gods to help us.

Raleigh   *So there was more than one you believed in?*

Marie   Yes.

Raleigh   *What did they tell you God looked like?*

Marie   Just like the heaven, the sun, like a light.

Raleigh   *Like a light?*

Marie   Up in the sky and all the lights at night.

Raleigh   *You looked back at your body, correct?*

Marie   Yes.

Raleigh   *Are you still in pain?*

Marie   Yes.

Raleigh   *YOU ARE?*

Marie   It's hurting.

Raleigh   *Where did you go from there? Better yet, tell me when the pain stops.*

Marie   When I couldn't see my body anymore.

Raleigh   *So you hadn't totally died yet, had you?*

Marie   No.

Raleigh   *You had just left your body, but you were still in physical pain.*

Marie   Yes.

Raleigh   *Now the pain stopped. So you have truly passed on, haven't you?*

Marie   Yes.

Raleigh   *Where did you go from there? What did you see?*

Marie	God.
Raleigh	*Describe it to me, please.*
Marie	Water.
Raleigh	*Did you travel for a long time?*
Marie	Yes.
Raleigh	*Let's go to when you finally meet someone. Understand?*
Marie	Yes.
Raleigh	*Who did you see? Okay, it's getting very late tonight, so we have to travel a little faster. At one point I know that you met God, didn't you?*
Marie	I see a bright light.
Raleigh	*What color of light?*
Marie	White. I see a door.
Raleigh	*Tell me about the door. What did the door look like?*
Marie	A regular door. It was open.
Raleigh	*When you got through the door, what did you see?*
Marie	Strangers.
Raleigh	*Was there anyone you knew?*
Marie	My father.
Raleigh	*Your father?*
Marie	Yes.
Raleigh	*You haven't seen him for a while?*
Marie	No.
Raleigh	*How is he dressed?*
Marie	He has something on like a dress.
Raleigh	*What color is it?*
Marie	White. Everything is white. Beautiful.
Raleigh	*Are there other people there?*
Marie	My mother.
Raleigh	*Dressed the same way?*
Marie	Yes, standing by a tree though. It's huge. There's the light.

Raleigh	*Is it a bright light?*
Marie	Yes.
Raleigh	*What is your family telling you?*
Marie	[Softly.] "We hear you're going further. You'll see peace."
Raleigh	*Was it only people that look like you there, or are there white people as well?*
Marie	All kinds.
Raleigh	*All dressed the same?*
Marie	Yes.
Raleigh	*How are you dressed now?*
Marie	In white.
Raleigh	*You're in white? Let's go to where you were given these white clothes that you wear, okay?*
Marie	Yes.
Raleigh	*At one point someone gave you the white clothes. When they gave them to you, what did they say? Who gave you the white clothes?*
Marie	A man.
Raleigh	*Describe the man.*
Marie	He has like a lot of light on … around a lot of white light.
Raleigh	*More than the others?*
Marie	Yes. He looks friendly, a friendly person, I think.
Raleigh	*Big man? Small man? Short? Fat?*
Marie	Normal.
Raleigh	*How close are you? Very close?*
Marie	Not that close. He give me some clothes on the ground. I look at them. "It's safe," He says. "You are safe now."
Raleigh	*Okay.*
Marie	I pick it up.

Raleigh	*Let's go exactly word for word. What did He tell you? As He says it, repeat it.*
Marie	"Come here. You are safe, My child."
Raleigh	*Okay.*
Marie	"You don't need those clothes that you have. Here everybody is the same. You have no hunger."
Raleigh	*There is no hunger?*
Marie	Yes. "You can rest."
Raleigh	*Is that all He said?*
Marie	Yes.
Raleigh	*Is He like you?*
Marie	No, kind of different.
Raleigh	*How is He different?*
Marie	I don't know.
Raleigh	*Okay, describe the man as you would see Him. Can you see His eyes?*
Marie	The light is too bright.
Raleigh	*Okay.*
Marie	I can see His mouth. He's smiling.
Raleigh	*He's smiling. Did He at any point touch you?*
Marie	Lightly, it was warm.
Raleigh	*It was warm. So are you afraid anymore?*
Marie	No.
Raleigh	*Are you afraid of me now?*
Marie	No.
Raleigh	*You know you have died?*
Marie	Yes.
Raleigh	*You know you have gone to heaven?*
Marie	Yes.
Raleigh	*Is that where you are talking to me from now?*
Marie	Yes.

Raleigh	*Why did you come to help Marie? You have been with her a long time, haven't you?*
Marie	Yes, from when she was a baby. She must get strong.
Raleigh	*She must get strong? Is that correct?*
Marie	Yes.
Raleigh	*Why Marie?*
Marie	She was a baby too early.
Raleigh	*Too early?*
Marie	She needed somebody who can help her.
Raleigh	*Were you shown Marie?*
Marie	Yes.
Raleigh	*Who showed you her?*
Marie	My father.
Raleigh	*What did he say?*
Marie	Help her because she needs your strength.
Raleigh	*But she is a white woman.*
Marie	Yes.
Raleigh	*Does that matter anymore?*
Marie	No, not anymore. She has a good heart.
Raleigh	*She has a good heart.*
Marie	Yes.
Raleigh	*Have you learned from Marie?*
Marie	Yes.
Raleigh	*What have you learned?*
Marie	Not all white people are bad, and if you be nice, they will be nice to you.
Raleigh	*Were you told that you had to learn a lesson?*
Marie	Yes.
Raleigh	*Who told you that?*
Marie	By God.
Raleigh	*By God. What did He tell you?*
Marie	Don't be … don't … I don't know how to say it.

Raleigh   *Okay, just repeat what you were told.*

Marie   "Don't blame the white people for losing your child. Don't blame the white people for losing your father. You must learn to don't blame other people for your own mistakes. Keep looking now. You are going to help the white baby until she dies."

Raleigh   *Until she dies?*

Marie   Yes.

Raleigh   *Have you done that?*

Marie   Yes, I'm trying.

Raleigh   *Ha-ha-ha, kind of a culture shock.*

Marie   Yes, it's different.

Raleigh   *But you have been approached again, haven't you? Someone has come to you and said we would talk. Our paths were meant to cross, weren't they?*

Marie   Somebody told me people are talking about, and want to know about, me. I must tell my story so you can tell your story.

Raleigh   *Okay, explain it a little more.*

Marie   Somebody told me there would be a person ask how I died. I have to tell him so he can pass it on to somebody else.

Raleigh   *Okay.*

Marie   You have to tell other people to learn about what happened.

Raleigh   *About what happens after you die?*

Marie   Both sides. What happened back then, what happened back then.

Raleigh   *Yes.*

Marie   They don't have to blame other people about your own mistakes.

Raleigh   *Okay.*

Marie	That is an important lesson.
Raleigh	*That's important.*
Marie	Yes.
Raleigh	*Who told you I would come and ask these questions?*
Marie	The man with the light.
Raleigh	*The man with the light said that?*
Marie	Yes.
Raleigh	*And He said I would tell that story?*
Marie	He said, "Someone would come soon to tell about your story. You must help him."
Raleigh	*So do you know my story I'm doing? Have you been shown what I'm doing?*
Marie	No.
Raleigh	*You just knew it would happen?*
Marie	Yes.
Raleigh	*But you didn't know it would be me?*
Marie	No.
Raleigh	*After we started talking, did you realize it?*
Marie	Yes, I feel good.
Raleigh	*You feel good?*
Marie	Yes, I had a sign it feels good to talk.
Raleigh	*What is a simple name I can call you since Mambella is a little formal?*
Marie	They also call me Go With the Wind.
Raleigh	*Go With the Wind?*
Marie	Yes, I go with the wind.
Raleigh	*Ha-ha, you go with the wind a lot?*
Marie	Yes.
Raleigh	*Okay, Go With the Wind it will be.*

EPISODE 7

◆ A Sandy Road ◆

As I WAS going through past tapes in order to do this book, I came across this tape. Most of the time I try to label and date my tapes, but this one had just slipped by. It must have been one of those sessions which went into the wee hours of the morning. At any rate, it was shelved and forgotten until now.

I met Rick and his family many years ago, but it seems like yesterday. Our families have seen the best of times as well as the worst. Their only son passed away recently. As a pallbearer, I had the honor of helping lay him to rest.

I would like to dedicate this episode in loving memory of Heath Andrew. He will always be with us.

Rick and Carrie, I am very pleased you allowed us to be a part of your life.

Raleigh	*Okay, now we are going to another time, another place, before you were born. This is another time, another place you know nothing of, before you were born. What do you see?*
Rick	I'm just wandering on a road. [Very softly.]
Raleigh	*What?*
Rick	There's a lot of sand.
Raleigh	*Where are you in relation to the sand?*
Rick	There's like this crater, and I'm in the bottom of it. I'm walking across it.
Raleigh	*Are you alone?*

Rick	I'm not with anybody else.
Raleigh	*Please describe yourself. What do you look like?*
Rick	I'm kind of dark-skinned, brown. I have like a robe, but it's dirty. There's … my head is covered with something, too. It's white and brown. It's dirty, too.
Raleigh	*Alright.*
Rick	I have … kind of looks … kind of looks … like a big stick. I don't know what you call them, but I've seen it before.
Raleigh	*Like a staff?*
Rick	Yes, it's kind of fancy looking. It's pretty tall.
Raleigh	*How old are you?*
Rick	I'm not really sure. Sometimes he looks old and sometimes he doesn't look old. I can't see the face real well because it's dirty.
Raleigh	*Okay. Continue on, but start to blend in and become one with that person. Okay?*
Rick	Okay.
Raleigh	*Where are you going?*
Rick	I think I'm lost. I'm looking for everyone else, I think.
Raleigh	*What do you see?*
Rick	It's hot!
Raleigh	*Do you have water or any other kind of drink?*
Rick	No. I'm just wandering around. I'm not sure I know where I'm going.
Raleigh	*Is this the heat of the day?*
Rick	The sun is behind me.
Raleigh	*Is it going down or coming up?*
Rick	It's going down.
Raleigh	*Let's continue on.*
Rick	Alright.

Raleigh	*What's happening now?*
Rick	I'm going to a city of tents.
Raleigh	*What about it? Are you there?*
Rick	I'm almost there.
Raleigh	*It's getting toward evening?*
Rick	Yes. [Keeps wetting his lips.]
Raleigh	*Are you thirsty?*
Rick	Very!
Raleigh	*What's your name?*
Rick	I'm not sure.
Raleigh	*Okay, did you make it to the city?*
Rick	No.
Raleigh	*What happened?*
Rick	I went into my tent.
Raleigh	*Is this before the city?*
Rick	It looks like a circus. The tents have stripes, all different stripes.
Raleigh	*Okay, what is going on at the tents?*
Rick	At my tent, nothing.
Raleigh	*Are you alone?*
Rick	Yes, there's a striped blanket on the floor.
Raleigh	*What do you do there?*
Rick	Just sleep.
Raleigh	*Did you get a drink?*
Rick	No, not at this time.
Raleigh	*Did you wake up the next day?*
Rick	I can see the sun.
Raleigh	*Okay, are you alone?*
Rick	Yes.
Raleigh	*Let's come to a time you are talking to someone. Okay?*
Rick	Okay.
Raleigh	*Who are you talking to?*

Rick	A boy with the water.
Raleigh	*A boy with the water?*
Rick	Yes.
Raleigh	*What are you telling him?*
Rick	I need water.
Raleigh	*What does he say?*
Rick	Rations.
Raleigh	*Rations?*
Rick	Rations. I don't think there is too much left.
Raleigh	*Did you get a drink?*
Rick	No.
Raleigh	*Why?*
Rick	I'm going to wait.
Raleigh	*Okay, let's go to someone who knows you. Okay?*
Rick	Alright.
Raleigh	*Who is it who knows you?*
Rick	An old woman.
Raleigh	*What does she call you?*
Rick	I don't know.
Raleigh	*What do you call her?*
Rick	I don't know.
Raleigh	*Okay, what is going on right now?*
Rick	It's dark. I talk to this lady, but I don't know what her name is.
Raleigh	*Are you new to this area?*
Rick	Yes, but I've seen this woman before.
Raleigh	*How old are you?*
Rick	Early 30s.
Raleigh	*Alright, do you have a wife?*
Rick	No.
Raleigh	*Do you have a family, like brothers or sisters?*
Rick	No.

Raleigh	*What is your name? What do you keep hearing?*
Rick	Ahk … Ahk … Ahkmaid … AHKMAD.
Raleigh	*Ahkmad? Is that it?*
Rick	AHKMAD, yes.
Raleigh	*Now you are going to step into Ahkmad's shoes. Okay?*
Rick	Okay.
Raleigh	*You will relive his life for a while. Alright?*
Rick	Alright.
Raleigh	*I am now speaking directly to Ahkmad. Understand?*
Rick	Yes.
Raleigh	*Now where are you going?*
Rick	We move to a new place to set up.
Raleigh	*Okay.*
Rick	We want a home.
Raleigh	*You want a home?*
Rick	Yes.
Raleigh	*What is your nationality? What religion?*
Rick	Hebrew.
Raleigh	*Hebrew, okay. So you are just wandering like a nomad?*
Rick	We are looking for a place we can make a home.
Raleigh	*Are you following someone?*
Rick	There are a lot of us, miles and miles and miles of people walking, horses and animals.
Raleigh	*Do you know a good deal of them?*
Rick	No.
Raleigh	*Where are you coming from?*
Rick	We were ran out.
Raleigh	*Where were you ran out of?*
Rick	Down the river.
Raleigh	*By the river? Who ran you out?*
Rick	The Romans.
Raleigh	*Okay. Are the Romans mean?*

Rick	Yes, you don't look at them.
Raleigh	*You don't look at them? What happens if you do look?*
Rick	Anything can happen.
Raleigh	*Anything?*
Rick	They can beat you and take your property, wife, kids, anything, if you look at them.
Raleigh	*Who is your leader ... or the person leading this band of people?*
Rick	I don't think there's one.
Raleigh	*Is there a main person that people listen to?*
Rick	No.
Raleigh	*Who do you go to for guidance?*
Rick	We all gather in prayer. Everybody.
Raleigh	*What is the year? Has a man named Jesus been born yet?*
Rick	Yes.
Raleigh	*Has He died yet?*
Rick	I don't think so.
Raleigh	*Why? What makes you think that?*
Rick	I think that's where we are going. That's where we are going.
Raleigh	*Where is it?*
Rick	Not far.
Raleigh	*Not far?*
Rick	No.
Raleigh	*Okay, let's come ahead in time.*
Rick	Alright.
Raleigh	*Did you see Jesus?*
Rick	No. [Very restless.]
Raleigh	*What happened? Did something happen to you?*
Rick	No, they arrested Him!
Raleigh	*They arrested Him?*

Rick	That's what we are being told!
Raleigh	*Were you near Him when He was arrested?*
Rick	No, I was a distance away.
Raleigh	*Was it a long distance?*
Rick	No.
Raleigh	*How do you know He had been arrested?*
Rick	Rumors!
Raleigh	*When the rumors came around, what was said?*
Rick	They are afraid to believe, scared.
Raleigh	*Do you believe?*
Rick	I believe!
Raleigh	*What do you believe of Him?*
Rick	He must be the Prophet!
Raleigh	*What makes you think that?*
Rick	Miracles!
Raleigh	*Have you seen the miracles?*
Rick	No.
Raleigh	*Okay, let's come ahead in time farther.*
Rick	Alright.
Raleigh	*They have arrested Him, correct?*
Rick	Yes.
Raleigh	*Did you see Him at all?*
Rick	No.
Raleigh	*You never got to see Him? Is that correct?*
Rick	No.
Raleigh	*What about your life? Where did your life lead you? Did you grow old?*
Rick	No.
Raleigh	*What happened to you?*
Rick	I was stoned.
Raleigh	*You were stoned? Why?*
Rick	I believe!

Raleigh	*Which was what?*
Rick	That Christ is God's Son!
Raleigh	*Who stoned you?*
Rick	Mobs.
Raleigh	*Was it your own people?*
Rick	Not the group that I traveled with.
Raleigh	*Were they also stoned?*
Rick	Some.
Raleigh	*Why did they pick you? What did you do?*
Rick	I cried.
Raleigh	*You cried? At what?*
Rick	At Christ's death, I cried.
Raleigh	*Did you see Him crucified?*
Rick	I saw Him there.
Raleigh	*You saw Him there? Where?*
Rick	After. He's still on the cross.
Raleigh	*Were there a lot of people there?*
Rick	For a while.
Raleigh	*Did they stone you before they let Him down?*
Rick	They never took Him down. I was made to leave.
Raleigh	*Where were you at? Were you close at the crucifixion? Or a distance away?*
Rick	I was close.
Raleigh	*Very close?*
Rick	I'd touch Him if I could. It's the cross.
Raleigh	*Alright, who told you to leave? Is this where you cried?*
Rick	Yes.
Raleigh	*Were you instantly arrested then?*
Rick	No.
Raleigh	*When were you arrested? Were you arrested?*
Rick	No.
Raleigh	*Did you stay there?*

Rick	No, they made me turn around and go back to town.
Raleigh	*Yes?*
Rick	And … [pause] … it's terrible.
Raleigh	*What?*
Rick	What they did.
Raleigh	*To you?*
Rick	No, what they did to Christ.
Raleigh	*In what way?*
Rick	Called Him liar, false prophet.
Raleigh	*This was your own people doing this?*
Rick	No, came a long ways.
Raleigh	*These people did?*
Rick	No, I did.
Raleigh	*Oh, you did, okay. The people you were traveling with, did they make it with you?*
Rick	Some.
Raleigh	*Are these the ones that were saying these things? False prophet and things such as that?*
Rick	No, the people of the town.
Raleigh	*It was the people of the town, correct?*
Rick	Yes, then they surrounded us. Some got away.
Raleigh	*But you didn't?*
Rick	No. They started yelling at us, "Fool, fool." There's a hole in the ground. They pushed me in, calling us names.
Raleigh	*What did they call you?*
Rick	"Jew." [Softly.]
Raleigh	*Please say it again.*
Rick	It's hard to pronounce.
Raleigh	*Say it the best you can.*
Rick	"Jew pit, Jew pits zu."

Raleigh	*A Jew pit zu? Is that correct?*
Rick	"Jew pit zu." Yes, I think that's right.
Raleigh	*What does that mean?*
Rick	A coward.
Raleigh	*A coward? I don't understand why they would call you a coward.*
Rick	I don't know.
Raleigh	*What were they saying you were being cowardly about?*
Rick	It's all backwards.
Raleigh	*What?*
Rick	It's all so backwards.
Raleigh	*What is all backwards?*
Rick	I'm not sure what or who they worship, and because of who I worship, they call me coward.
Raleigh	*Okay, let's come to the time where they killed you. Alright?*
Rick	Alright.
Raleigh	*Was it the town people who killed you?*
Rick	Yes.
Raleigh	*By this time, had Jesus already died?*
Rick	Yes.
Raleigh	*Jesus died before you, correct?*
Rick	Yes.
Raleigh	*When they stoned you with the stones, did this kill you?*
Rick	No, not yet. I was dragged.
Raleigh	*You were dragged?*
Rick	Dragged by a horse.
Raleigh	*Okay, dragged by a horse. Where?*
Rick	I was dragged into the river.
Raleigh	*You were dragged into the river? Why?*
Rick	I don't know.

Raleigh	*There was no reason?*
Rick	No reason.
Raleigh	*Is that where your body laid then? Was it in the water?*
Rick	In the water and a little on land.
Raleigh	*At this point, have you died?*
Rick	Yes.
Raleigh	*You have. Alright, what happened to you after you died? Tell me what you see. Is this the same day Jesus died?*
Rick	I don't know if ....
Raleigh	*Okay, close, at least?*
Rick	Yes.
Raleigh	*Tell me what you see.*
Rick	It's dark.
Raleigh	*Yes?*
Rick	I'm going into a light. I'm here.
Raleigh	*You're where? Are you trying to understand how you have died but are still talking to me?*
Rick	Yes.
Raleigh	*Okay, let's go through, and you'll understand more. Let's go through what happened after you died, okay?*
Rick	Yes.
Raleigh	*I will tell you this before we continue on any farther: 2,000 years, almost, have passed by from your time to now. It is very hard for you to understand now. Okay? Almost 2,000 years. I am able to speak to you as if you were alive, 2,000 years later, because of Jesus dying on that cross. Okay?*
Rick	Yes.
Raleigh	*Now tell me what happened to you after you died.*
Rick	I feel released.
Raleigh	*Okay, are you at peace?*

Rick	Yes.
Raleigh	*Tell me when you first see someone. Okay?*
Rick	Okay.
Raleigh	*This is after you have died. Who is it that you see?*
Rick	Umm, nobody.
Raleigh	*What are you seeing?*
Rick	I feel ....
Raleigh	*A field?*
Rick	No, I feel ... helpless.
Raleigh	*You feel helpless? Why?*
Rick	No control.
Raleigh	*We'll continue on until you meet someone. Understand? Who is it that you see?*
Rick	Colors.
Raleigh	*Colors?*
Rick	Bright colors. Beautiful.
Raleigh	*Are you entering into those colors?*
Rick	They are all around.
Raleigh	*Who do you see? Who is it?*
Rick	The Lord's hand. [Softly.]
Raleigh	*Say it again, please.*
Rick	The hands ... holds a hand out in front of me ... bright clouds ... I can't ....
Raleigh	*When do you see the Lord? Can you see Him now?*
Rick	Yes, through the light.
Raleigh	*Through the light?*
Rick	Yes. He seems to be farther away than He is.
Raleigh	*What does He look like?*
Rick	Bright, eyes pure.
Raleigh	*He has pure eyes?*
Rick	He's holding His hands out. He seems so far away.
Raleigh	*Okay, is this the same individual you saw on the cross?*

Rick	Yes.
Raleigh	*Okay, so now you know that was the truth then?*
Rick	Yes, I believe. "I am the Lord thy God."
Raleigh	*This is what you are being told?*
Rick	"I am the Lord thy God." He looks ....
Raleigh	*He looks at what?*
Rick	He looks as diamonds, jewels, so beautiful.
Raleigh	*What else does He tell you?*
Rick	"Your suffering ...."
Raleigh	*What?*
Rick	"… is ...." He doesn't speak, but I can hear Him. I don't feel myself.
Raleigh	*Are you a little scared?*
Rick	A little.
Raleigh	*Does He give the feeling you should be scared, or is it friendly and warm?*
Rick	Like nothing .... I'm not scared.
Raleigh	*What else does He tell you? Was that all He told you?*
Rick	"I am the Lord thy God. You have not wandered from thy faith nor shed tears in vain." That's all He says.
Raleigh	*Does He continue to talk to you?*
Rick	"It's all right. Don't be afraid. It's all over."

EPISODE 8

◆ An Old Town ◆

TAMMY CAME TO my home one evening in 1995 with a group of people interested in being regressed. After watching a few others, she wanted to try it herself.

I chose this story because Tammy's helper, Melissa, was an everyday individual who lived a quiet life and then died. It shows that even though you may not have made great waves — or even small ripples — in the sea of life, God still watches over all of us and is waiting for each of us on the other side.

Raleigh	*We're drifting now, back to before you were born. We're going back, back, back to another time, another place. A place that you know nothing of. I want you to tell me what the first thing is that you see. Do you understand? What do you see?*
Tammy	Trees.
Raleigh	*What kind of trees?*
Tammy	Elm trees.
Raleigh	*Okay, are they little ones or big ones?*
Tammy	Big ones.
Raleigh	*Where are you in relation to these trees?*
Tammy	Above them.
Raleigh	*Above them, alright. Doing what?*
Tammy	I don't know ... just floating.

Raleigh	*Okay, let's go back farther, before that. We're drifting farther back in that day. In fact, we're going to go farther back in your life. Do you understand? We're going back to before you were floating above the elm trees. What do you see?*
Tammy	An old town.
Raleigh	*What about the town? Describe the town to me.*
Tammy	Lots of horses … and wagons.
Raleigh	*Okay, and where are you in relation to these?*
Tammy	In the center.
Raleigh	*Of the town?*
Tammy	Yeah.
Raleigh	*How old are you?*
Tammy	I think about 21.
Raleigh	*About 21? Describe yourself.*
Tammy	I have a long dress. My hair's curly.
Raleigh	*What color?*
Tammy	Blonde.
Raleigh	*Alright, what do people call you? What is your name?*
Tammy	Melissa.
Raleigh	*Melissa, alright. What year is it, Melissa?*
Tammy	I don't know.
Raleigh	*Okay, that's alright. Why are you in town, Melissa?*
Tammy	I'm just walking.
Raleigh	*Where are you walking from?*
Tammy	Across the street.
Raleigh	*What was across the street?*
Tammy	I think a grocery store.
Raleigh	*Do you have packages in your hands?*
Tammy	No.
Raleigh	*Alright, what were you doing in the grocery store?*
Tammy	Looking.

Raleigh	*Looking, at what?*
Tammy	Jars.
Raleigh	*At jars? Were you wanting to buy some jars or just looking at them?*
Tammy	Just looking.
Raleigh	*Do you think jars are neat?*
Tammy	Yeah.
Raleigh	*Okay. Why, what is the attraction with jars?*
Tammy	Put stuff in 'em.
Raleigh	*You put stuff in them, ha-ha, okay. Do you do canning?*
Tammy	No.
Raleigh	*No, you put other things in them, is that right? Like what?*
Tammy	Jewelry.
Raleigh	*Do you have a lot of jewelry?*
Tammy	No, not really.
Raleigh	*Okay, what color are these jars?*
Tammy	Brown.
Raleigh	*Alright. Are they like a quart jar? Is that what they are?*
Tammy	Yeah.
Raleigh	*Do they have lids? What kind of a lid do they have?*
Tammy	It's got a clasp on it.
Raleigh	*Okay, is it a glass top?*
Tammy	Yeah.
Raleigh	*These are like fruit jars?*
Tammy	Yeah.
Raleigh	*They've got like a wire clip that goes over the top, don't they?*
Tammy	Yeah.
Raleigh	*Alright, so where are you going to now? You left the store, and where are you headed?*
Tammy	Across the street.

Raleigh	*To do what?*
Tammy	I don't know. I'm just walking across the street.
Raleigh	*Okay, do you live in this town, or outside of town?*
Tammy	No, I live outside.
Raleigh	*Are you married?*
Tammy	No.
Raleigh	*Do you have brothers and sisters?*
Tammy	No.
Raleigh	*Do you live alone?*
Tammy	Yeah.
Raleigh	*What about your parents? What happened to your parents?*
Tammy	They're gone.
Raleigh	*Have they been gone a long time?*
Tammy	Yeah.
Raleigh	*Where is this town, Melissa? What's the name of it?*
Tammy	I don't know.
Raleigh	*As you're heading into town, is there a sign that says what the name of the town is? Is there a sign on any of the stores, or a bank, saying what the name is?*
Tammy	No.
Raleigh	*What do people call the town?*
Tammy	New Guinea, or something like that.
Raleigh	*New Guinea?*
Tammy	Yeah.
Raleigh	*Okay, what country are you in?*
Tammy	I don't know.
Raleigh	*Do you speak with an accent? As I speak to you, do you hear me sounding different than the people of your town?*
Tammy	No.
Raleigh	*Not in language, but in accent?*

Tammy	No.
Raleigh	*What country are you in? Just let it come to you, alright?*
Tammy	I don't know.
Raleigh	*Okay, let's continue on. Your family has been gone for some time, is that correct?*
Tammy	Yeah.
Raleigh	*And you live alone?*
Tammy	Umm hmm.
Raleigh	*And you're 21, do you have friends?*
Tammy	No.
Raleigh	*What do you do for a living?*
Tammy	Sew.
Raleigh	*You sew, alright. Do you have your own home?*
Tammy	Yeah, I think so.
Raleigh	*You do, okay, was it your parents' home?*
Tammy	Yeah.
Raleigh	*It was? What did your parents die from?*
Tammy	I think a wagon accident.
Raleigh	*A wagon accident, is that correct?*
Tammy	Yes.
Raleigh	*A wagon turned over?*
Tammy	Yes.
Raleigh	*And they were both on it? And it killed both of them?*
Tammy	Yes.
Raleigh	*How old were you when this happened?*
Tammy	I was 15.
Raleigh	*Fifteen, so it's been kind of a hard life for you then, hasn't it? Did you go to school?*
Tammy	Sometimes.
Raleigh	*Did you live on a farm?*
Tammy	Yes.

Raleigh	*Did you farm the farm?*
Tammy	Not after my dad was gone.
Raleigh	*Okay, who farmed your farm?*
Tammy	No one.
Raleigh	*You didn't try to rent the land out or sell it?*
Tammy	No.
Raleigh	*Was it a very big farm?*
Tammy	Umm, yeah.
Raleigh	*It was? How did you pay for your parents to be buried? Was there money to do that?*
Tammy	Yeah.
Raleigh	*Okay. Did you have to do it yourself?*
Tammy	I didn't bury them.
Raleigh	*You didn't bury them? Who did?*
Tammy	Some man did it.
Raleigh	*Did you have a funeral for them?*
Tammy	Yes.
Raleigh	*You did? Did you pay for the funeral?*
Tammy	Yes.
Raleigh	*What did the funeral cost you? Did you have gravestones made for them?*
Tammy	No.
Raleigh	*Why?*
Tammy	We didn't have enough money.
Raleigh	*Was there a marker put up?*
Tammy	No.
Raleigh	*Was a funeral expensive?*
Tammy	Yeah.
Raleigh	*What did it cost you? I don't expect you to understand at this point in time, but these things have already happened. What did it cost you?*
Tammy	Two dollars.

Raleigh	*Alright. Where was the funeral held at?*
Tammy	By our home.
Raleigh	*Did people come to it?*
Tammy	Just a few.
Raleigh	*Did you have relatives — aunts, uncles, cousins?*
Tammy	No.
Raleigh	*You were just alone?*
Tammy	Yes.
Raleigh	*Alright, do you trust me, Melissa?*
Tammy	Yes.
Raleigh	*Okay. Did you have a family Bible, Melissa?*
Tammy	Yes.
Raleigh	*Did you write the dates in the family Bible?*
Tammy	Yes, I did.
Raleigh	*What did you write as the date?*
Tammy	I don't ... 18 something.
Raleigh	*Take a look at it, alright? I know this is a bit painful for you. I understand that. But things will soon become very beautiful for you, okay? What was the date?*
Tammy	Eighteen something.
Raleigh	*What was the something? Look at the page.*
Tammy	Seventeen.
Raleigh	*1817? And what were the names that you inscribed?*
Tammy	George and Dorothy Graber.
Raleigh	*And is your name in the book?*
Tammy	No.
Raleigh	*Because you hadn't passed on, had you?*
Tammy	No.
Raleigh	*Was your birthday written in there?*
Tammy	No.
Raleigh	*No? Not on that page, anyhow?*
Tammy	No.

Raleigh	*Okay, so your name is Melissa Graber?*
Tammy	Umm hmm.
Raleigh	*Is it G-R-A-B-E-R, or has it got two b's in it?*
Tammy	No.
Raleigh	*Okay, G-R-A-B-E-R?*
Tammy	Umm hmm, yes.
Raleigh	*Okay. My name is Raleigh. Nice to meet you, Melissa. I know that times are hard for you, but you probably had pleasant times, as well. Let's go to a pleasant time. Tell me about it.*
Tammy	I was younger.
Raleigh	*You were younger? Your parents were alive? Okay, tell me about it. What were you doing that day?*
Tammy	Playing with sticks.
Raleigh	*Ha-ha, okay, what were you doing with the sticks?*
Tammy	Rolling them.
Raleigh	*Little sticks or big ones?*
Tammy	Little ones.
Raleigh	*Okay, what were you rolling them on?*
Tammy	The ground.
Raleigh	*Rolling them with your hands or with your feet?*
Tammy	With my hands.
Raleigh	*Why is this such a nice day for you?*
Tammy	I'm playing.
Raleigh	*You're playing, is this something unusual?*
Tammy	Oh … no.
Raleigh	*It's just a pleasant day?*
Tammy	Yeah.
Raleigh	*Is your mom or your dad there with you?*
Tammy	My dad's outside.
Raleigh	*Your dad's outside with you? Is he talking to you?*
Tammy	He's … he's brushing the horse.

Raleigh	*Is he talking to you?*
Tammy	Just laughing at me.
Raleigh	*For playing with sticks? What's he saying, or is he just laughing?*
Tammy	Just laughing.
Raleigh	*What's your dad look like?*
Tammy	Gray hair, got a hat on. Shirt … a long-sleeve shirt.
Raleigh	*Is it warm or cold out?*
Tammy	It's warm.
Raleigh	*Are you having fun?*
Tammy	Yeah.
Raleigh	*Let's go to a pleasant memory with your mom.*
Tammy	We're cooking.
Raleigh	*What's she cooking that you like?*
Tammy	She's … I guess she's boiling water.
Raleigh	*To do what?*
Tammy	Cook vegetables, or something.
Raleigh	*What's your favorite food?*
Tammy	Carrots.
Raleigh	*You like carrots. Cooked carrots or raw carrots?*
Tammy	Raw carrots.
Raleigh	*Okay, is your mom talking to you?*
Tammy	Yeah.
Raleigh	*What's she saying?*
Tammy	Showing me how to chop the carrots.
Raleigh	*Okay. How is your mom dressed?*
Tammy	Long dress on … her hair's up.
Raleigh	*What color is her hair?*
Tammy	Brown.
Raleigh	*Is she pretty?*
Tammy	Umm hmm.
Raleigh	*How old is she?*

Tammy	I think she's 42.
Raleigh	*How old are you right then?*
Tammy	Five.
Raleigh	*She was pretty old when she had you, then. Isn't that right?*
Tammy	Yeah.
Raleigh	*Did she have any other children?*
Tammy	No.
Raleigh	*We're going to come back now to the day you were in that town. Do you understand? What was the name of the town?*
Tammy	New Guinea.
Raleigh	*And what country was it in? [Long pause.] Was it in the United States? Did you celebrate the Fourth of July?*
Tammy	No.
Raleigh	*Did anyone celebrate the Fourth of July? Independence Day?*
Tammy	I don't think so.
Raleigh	*No, okay. So what country are you in?*
Tammy	I don't know.
Raleigh	*Can you read?*
Tammy	Yes.
Raleigh	*Alright, have you read about your country? Did you study your country in school?*
Tammy	No.
Raleigh	*Did you ever see a picture or a map that showed your country?*
Tammy	No.
Raleigh	*How about a newspaper? Have you ever read a newspaper?*
Tammy	Yes.

Raleigh	*What was the name of the paper?*
Tammy	I don't know.
Raleigh	*That's alright. Let's come up to the day that you were in the town. Did something happen to you when you were trying to cross the street?*
Tammy	I almost got ran over.
Raleigh	*Did you get run over?*
Tammy	No.
Raleigh	*Why did you almost get hit in the street, didn't you see him?*
Tammy	They were so fast.
Raleigh	*They were traveling fast?*
Tammy	Yeah.
Raleigh	*They didn't slow up for you?*
Tammy	No.
Raleigh	*Was it a wagon or people on horses?*
Tammy	It was a wagon.
Raleigh	*Alright. Did something happen to you that day?*
Tammy	No.
Raleigh	*Okay, let's go up to the time … you seem awfully worried, why? I see, like a troubled expression on your face, why is that? [No answer.] Are you wondering how I am able to talk to you?*
Tammy	Yeah.
Raleigh	*You are?*
Tammy	Yeah.
Raleigh	*Okay. Let me explain it, alright? Something happened to you many, many years ago. Time has passed. Now, we're going to go to the time in which you lost your life. Do you understand? What happened that day?*
Tammy	I got sick. [She starts scratching her right arm.]
Raleigh	*You got sick? Okay. Does your arm itch?*

Tammy	A little.
Raleigh	*Okay, why are you scratching your arm? Is there a reason?*
Tammy	There's a rash, or something.
Raleigh	*There's a rash, okay. What were you sick from? Had you been sick a long period of time?*
Tammy	For a while.
Raleigh	*Okay, how old are you?*
Tammy	Twenty-eight.
Raleigh	*You're 28. Did you ever marry?*
Tammy	No.
Raleigh	*Did you have a boyfriend?*
Tammy	No.
Raleigh	*You never wished to get married and have children?*
Tammy	Sometimes.
Raleigh	*You never met anyone that you liked?*
Tammy	Umm … yeah.
Raleigh	*But nothing serious?*
Tammy	No.
Raleigh	*And you're now 28, is that right?*
Tammy	Yes.
Raleigh	*Had you been sick for very long?*
Tammy	Yeah.
Raleigh	*How long?*
Tammy	A month.
Raleigh	*Alright, what were your symptoms?*
Tammy	Fever, then a rash and a bad cough.
Raleigh	*Okay, did you go to a doctor at all?*
Tammy	No.
Raleigh	*Are there other people in the town that are sick like you?*
Tammy	I think so.

Raleigh	*Have you heard of this illness before?*
Tammy	No.
Raleigh	*Have you seen people with the symptoms?*
Tammy	With the rash.
Raleigh	*What does the rash look like? Is it just on your arm?*
Tammy	It's red and … no, it's on my legs.
Raleigh	*It's on your legs, as well?*
Tammy	Yeah.
Raleigh	*Okay, let's step back in time. What actually caused this illness? Let's go to the exact point of what caused it. Do you understand? What actually caused it?*
Tammy	I don't know. I just got sick.
Raleigh	*Was it big spots of rash?*
Tammy	Yes.
Raleigh	*Alright, you had been sick for about a month. Were you alone?*
Tammy	Yeah.
Raleigh	*Are you in bed?*
Tammy	Yes.
Raleigh	*Have you been able to eat anything?*
Tammy	No.
Raleigh	*How long have you not been able to eat?*
Tammy	A … long time.
Raleigh	*Did you drink water?*
Tammy	Tried … I felt sick.
Raleigh	*Did you have a fever?*
Tammy	Yes.
Raleigh	*Alright, let's go up to the time that you did pass on. Was it because of this illness?*
Tammy	Yes.
Raleigh	*Okay, what happened after that? You passed on, and then what? What did you see?*

Tammy   I don't know … it just feels like I'm … floating or something.

Raleigh   *Did you see your body?*

Tammy   Yeah.

Raleigh   *Did anyone find you?*

Tammy   It just seems like there's people waiting.

Raleigh   *People waiting?*

Tammy   I think so.

Raleigh   *What do you mean "waiting"?*

Tammy   I think they're waiting for me.

Raleigh   *Oh! There's people waiting for you, as you are passing on. You're looking ahead, then?*

Tammy   Yeah.

Raleigh   *Alright. Who is waiting for you? Who meets you?*

Tammy   Some lady, she has gray hair.

Raleigh   *How is she dressed?*

Tammy   Umm … I really only can see her face.

Raleigh   *What does she tell you?*

Tammy   She doesn't talk; she just holds her arms out.

Raleigh   *And what's on her arms?*

Tammy   It looks like a robe-type thing.

Raleigh   *What color?*

Tammy   Bluish … blue.

Raleigh   *A bluish-type robe?*

Tammy   Yeah.

Raleigh   *Okay, do you go to her?*

Tammy   Yes.

Raleigh   *Okay, and then where does she take you?*

Tammy   It just feels like we're floating.

Raleigh   *Okay, let's go to what happens next. Did you see your parents?*

Tammy   Not yet.

Raleigh	*What happens next?*
Tammy	I just feel very calm.
Raleigh	*Okay, let's go to where something happens. I take it you did see your parents, is that correct?*
Tammy	She said I would.
Raleigh	*Have you seen them?*
Tammy	Getting ready to.
Raleigh	*Who sees you first, your mom or your dad?*
Tammy	My dad.
Raleigh	*How is he dressed?*
Tammy	He just looks normal.
Raleigh	*Normal clothes?*
Tammy	Yeah.
Raleigh	*And how is your mom dressed?*
Tammy	Normal.
Raleigh	*How are you dressed?*
Tammy	Some kind of a … white thing on.
Raleigh	*Like a robe?*
Tammy	Yeah.
Raleigh	*What did your dad say to you? Did he speak?*
Tammy	He smiled.
Raleigh	*Did you go to them?*
Tammy	We just embraced.
Raleigh	*You didn't speak?*
Tammy	No.
Raleigh	*And then what happened?*
Tammy	We had to say good-bye.
Raleigh	*You had to say good-bye?*
Tammy	They had to go.
Raleigh	*Okay. On your journey, before you received your white robe, what did you see?*

Tammy   The lady with the gray hair … she took me to another room … and I waited.

Raleigh   *Okay, and then what happened? You didn't have your white robe yet?*

Tammy   No.

Raleigh   *How did you receive the white robe?*

Tammy   They put it on me.

Raleigh   *Who is "they"?*

Tammy   Two men.

Raleigh   *Describe these men. How are they dressed?*

Tammy   In blue robes. They're … they're smiling.

Raleigh   *Are they telling you anything?*

Tammy   No.

Raleigh   *Alright, let's come ahead then. Were you shown anything after you received your robe? What do you see?*

Tammy   A big stone chair … it's white.

Raleigh   *Is anyone there?*

Tammy   Yes.

Raleigh   *Okay, describe this individual.*

Tammy   His robe is flowing … and He has real pretty blue eyes.

Raleigh   *Pretty blue eyes?*

Tammy   Yes, calming … very calming.

Raleigh   *How big of a man is this?*

Tammy   Oh! A big man!

Raleigh   *Are you afraid?*

Tammy   No!

Raleigh   *Are you very close?*

Tammy   Yes.

Raleigh   *Do you know who this is?*

Tammy   I think He is the King of the Kingdom.

Raleigh   *You think what?*

Tammy	This is the King of the Kingdom.
Raleigh	*Do you mean God, Himself?*
Tammy	I believe so.
Raleigh	*Does He say anything? Does He touch you?*
Tammy	He holds up His hands.
Raleigh	*How does He hold up His hands?*
Tammy	Like this. [Holds her arms out with palms up.]
Raleigh	*And what does He say?*
Tammy	"Bless you, child. You are safe."
Raleigh	*Did you say anything in return?*
Tammy	I just smiled.
Raleigh	*Are you happy?*
Tammy	Yes!
Raleigh	*Are you at peace?*
Tammy	Oh, yes!
Raleigh	*No pain?*
Tammy	No.
Raleigh	*And what else does He tell you?*
Tammy	That we shall speak again.
Raleigh	*And then what did He do?*
Tammy	Smiled!

EPISODE 9

◆ A Grassy Field ◆

JACK AND I met about seven years ago and have been good friends ever since. Jack is a teacher from the Chicago area. He is married and has two children.

Throughout the years of performing hypnosis, I have come across only four famous past lives. In those cases, I find it very interesting that these people usually disagree with the things that have been written about them. These cases show how a one-sided picture can be painted about an individual. The episode you are about to read is one such example.

This transcript is from the second time I put Jack under. Since we live several states apart, I had to wait quite a while for this session. Our paths don't cross as often as we would like. I sincerely hope that you, the reader, will appreciate the wait.

As with any session, there are always questions I think of after the individual has left. I am certain that you, too, will think of other questions that I could have asked. Please, bear in mind that we are asking questions from their perspectives, not a history book's. This format creates an entirely different manner in which questions are asked and answered.

After the first time he went under hypnosis, Jack wondered if what he saw was accurate or just his imagination. He was almost afraid to tell anyone about his session because he did not want people to think he was nuts. But I can't resist telling. After all, it's not every day that you can have a one-on-one conversation with the one and only Napoleon Bonaparte.

The only knowledge Jack had of Napoleon was what we all learn in school. As time passes, however, he has found that many of his mannerisms are identical to those of Napoleon. This is not uncommon. Many of my subjects notice personal similarities with their own helper. The difficulty with famous people lies with proving the case. We have found that if we dig deep enough, we can find that obscure fact that will prove the case.

Well, since I already let the cat out of the bag, let's begin our journey back to Napoleon's France. Remember, this is our second meeting, so the questions are a little different from time to time. With that final note, let's begin.

Raleigh	*We are now going to another time, another place before you were born. A place you know nothing of. What do you see?*
Jack	I see a field.
Raleigh	*What time of day is it that you see this field?*
Jack	[A little hesitant.] Early morning?
Raleigh	*Do you feel the sun is coming up?*
Jack	Yes, I do.
Raleigh	*Is it a pretty day, a hot day, cold, or what?*
Jack	It's a warm day.
Raleigh	*Okay, and what kind of field is it?*
Jack	Grass.
Raleigh	*You mean like a pasture? Not like a farm?*
Jack	No.
Raleigh	*Are you alone?*
Jack	Umm … I don't think so.
Raleigh	*You don't think so? Look around you.*
Jack	Okay.
Raleigh	*Do you see someone else around you?*
Jack	Yes!

Raleigh	*Who is it?*
Jack	Men, other men.
Raleigh	*Other men, okay. Do you know these men?*
Jack	Yes!
Raleigh	*Who are they?*
Jack	They are my men.
Raleigh	*They're your men, and when you say, "My men," what do you mean?*
Jack	I command them.
Raleigh	*What do they call you?*
Jack	Sire.
Raleigh	*Sire, okay. What do they call you as a formal name?*
Jack	I don't know what you mean.
Raleigh	*What is your formal name? Let me put it this way: what was your name given to you at birth?*
	[No answer.]
	What did your mother call you?
	[No answer.]
	Let's go to a time when your mother was talking to you, okay?
Jack	Okay.
Raleigh	*How old are you?*
Jack	Nine.
Raleigh	*Nine, okay. Now what are you doing?*
Jack	Uh, I see this building.
Raleigh	*Okay, is your mother talking to you?*
Jack	She's calling my name.
Raleigh	*What's she calling you?*
Jack	[Long pause.] She's calling, "Nabouleon."
Raleigh	*Nabouleon? Is that what she is saying?*
Jack	Yes!

Raleigh	*What were you doing that she called you by name? Were you doing something wrong?*
Jack	No.
Raleigh	*Okay then, what were you doing?*
Jack	I was just standing outside.
Raleigh	*Okay, let's go to what your mother was telling you. What did she say?*
Jack	I ... I can't seem to hear her.
Raleigh	*Okay, let's come back to the field once more. I take it this is several years later?*
Jack	Yes.
Raleigh	*How old are you now?*
Jack	Thirty-nine.
Raleigh	*You're 39. Okay, what are you doing?*
Jack	Just looking.
Raleigh	*At what?*
Jack	The field.
Raleigh	*Is the field in your country?*
Jack	No.
Raleigh	*Where is it?*
	[No answer.]
	Are you going to, or returning from, somewhere?
Jack	Both.
Raleigh	*On this day, what are you looking for?*
Jack	Nothing.
Raleigh	*Your men are behind you? Are you standing off by yourself?*
Jack	Off ... off by myself.
Raleigh	*What are you thinking about right now?*
Jack	How pretty it looks.
Raleigh	*So it's a pretty field?*
Jack	Yes.

Raleigh	*Have you had a lot of victories?*
Jack	Yes!
Raleigh	*What is your native country?*
Jack	France.
Raleigh	*France?*
Jack	That's where I live. That is my home.
Raleigh	*Are you in France now?*
Jack	No.
Raleigh	*Where are you? Without a totally accurate map, where do you estimate you are?*
Jack	As far as country?
Raleigh	*Yes.*
Jack	I'm not exactly sure of my exact location.
Raleigh	*Are you returning to France?*
Jack	Yes.
Raleigh	*Are you a long distance away from France now?*
Jack	We're close.
Raleigh	*How many days away are you?*
Jack	Hmm … two … yes, two days.
Raleigh	*Two days from home, okay.*
Jack	Two days to France.
Raleigh	*Okay, to France, but not to home.*
Jack	No.
Raleigh	*Where had you gone? Did you go somewhere to go into battle?*
Jack	No.
Raleigh	*So this was a peaceful trip?*
Jack	Yes.
Raleigh	*Why did you go?*
Jack	To talk.
Raleigh	*To who?*
Jack	I went to talk to our allies.

Raleigh	*Who are your allies?*
Jack	Russia, Austria, Prussia. Many, many other small states.
Raleigh	*Okay, who is your worst enemy at age 39?*
Jack	Britain.
Raleigh	*Britain is, why? Does Britain not like you, or you don't like Britain?*
Jack	They don't want me where I'm at.
Raleigh	*What do you mean by that? They don't want you as a leader?*
Jack	No.
Raleigh	*Is talking to me hard?*
Jack	No, no.
Raleigh	*So these conversations don't bother you?*
Jack	No.
Raleigh	*What is your favorite thing in life, over everything else?*
Jack	My wife!
Raleigh	*Your wife? So she is quite important to you? How would you express your feelings about your wife?*
Jack	I … I'm not sure I completely understand.
Raleigh	*If you could describe your wife, not just physically, but what she really means to you. What would you say?*
Jack	She's my life.
Raleigh	*She's your life, okay. Do you have children?*
Jack	No.
Raleigh	*Why?*
Jack	[Small chuckle.] Because she hasn't had any.
Raleigh	*These are questions I have to ask, okay?*
Jack	Okay.
Raleigh	*This is your story of your life as never done before. Do you have a problem with that?*

Jack	No.
Raleigh	*You now know this is our second meeting, don't you?*
Jack	Yes.
Raleigh	*Because of who you are, the one and only Napoleon, I have waited a long time for our second meeting. We have to understand why — in the future for you but now in my time — you were depicted as such a bad person.*
Jack	Umm, hmm. [Frowns.]
Raleigh	*I know you frowned at that, but that is how you are portrayed. This is your opportunity to answer some of these charges, okay?*
Jack	Okay.
Raleigh	*Why would future writers portray you as such a brutal, heartless individual? These were historians later on. Now, be honest with yourself. Did you do things which were brutal, that would give you such recognition?*
Jack	Ah, at times, yes, maybe.
Raleigh	*At times?*
Jack	Yes, at times.
Raleigh	*Why? We are trying to understand.*
Jack	That's what had to be done.
Raleigh	*I know you are thinking of at least one such event. Isn't this true?*
Jack	Yes.
Raleigh	*What took place?*
Jack	I am thinking of many.
Raleigh	*Okay, just pick one that would have portrayed you as such an evil person.*
Jack	It depends which side you're looking at it.

Raleigh	*I understand, but I know you have something in mind, don't you? Something you knew just wasn't quite right, but went on anyhow.*
Jack	Umm hmm. My soldiers pushed opposing soldiers into the water.
Raleigh	*Okay, what was so brutal about that?*
Jack	Because they were defenseless. They had no arms.
Raleigh	*The opposing soldiers had no arms? Were they soldiers?*
Jack	Yes.
Raleigh	*They had no weapons?*
Jack	They surrendered again.
Raleigh	*They surrendered?*
Jack	Yes.
Raleigh	*Then you had them pushed back into the water?*
Jack	Yes.
Raleigh	*Was it like a lake, or what?*
Jack	No, bigger.
Raleigh	*River?*
Jack	No, bigger.
Raleigh	*Ocean?*
Jack	Kind of like an ocean. It had waves.
Raleigh	*Kind of like a sea? A gulf?*
Jack	Yes! Yes!
Raleigh	*Was it just on the banks, a cliff, or what was it?*
Jack	On a beach!
Raleigh	*Okay, what happened after the soldiers were in the water? Could they not swim?*
Jack	No. My soldiers pushed them out with their bayonets.
Raleigh	*Did any get away?*
Jack	I don't know.
Raleigh	*Was this a direct order from you?*

Jack	Yes.
Raleigh	*Why did you order that?*
Jack	I had let them go once and they came back to fight again.
Raleigh	*Okay, so this was the same group of soldiers? Do you know for a fact these were the same ones?*
Jack	Yes.
Raleigh	*You knew that. Okay, where were they from?*
Jack	I don't know their clothing. They are different, like baggy pants.
Raleigh	*What was your exact order?*
Jack	"Push them to the sea."
Raleigh	*Then what else?*
Jack	That was it.
Raleigh	*Although this was a brutal incident, I can almost understand what you did, if they came back to fight a second time.*
Jack	We were short on ammunition; that's why we couldn't shoot them. That's why they had to be pushed into the water.
Raleigh	*Although this is an order you didn't regret, though, is it?*
Jack	It had to be done.
Raleigh	*How about an order you later regretted? Did you ever give one of those that, after it was done, you knew it wasn't morally correct?*
Jack	Ah, I think at times … I think that my opinions, my beliefs, can be pretty strict.
Raleigh	*What is your opinion, your belief, that you are thinking right now?*

Jack	I am thinking in general, that there are times after, that I could have been more lenient about some things.
Raleigh	*Is there ever one that comes back to haunt you from time to time?*
Jack	Yes!
Raleigh	*And what might that be?*
Jack	The divorce of my wife.
Raleigh	*Why did you do it?*
Jack	Because I needed a son.
Raleigh	*Could she not have any?*
Jack	No.
Raleigh	*Did you talk to her about it?*
Jack	Meaning when? Anytime?
Raleigh	*Yes.*
Jack	Sure.
Raleigh	*What did she say?*
Jack	She would do what was best.
Raleigh	*So this is something you always regretted. Did you remarry?*
Jack	Yes.
Raleigh	*Did you have a son?*
Jack	Yes.
Raleigh	*Did you keep in contact with the ex-wife?*
Jack	Yes! Yes!
Raleigh	*How many children did you have?*
Jack	By my wife?
Raleigh	*Yes.*
Jack	One.
Raleigh	*Did you have other women? Other children?*
Jack	Yes.
Raleigh	*You didn't consider them sons?*

Jack	Yes, but they couldn't rule.
Raleigh	*Did people know they were your children?*
Jack	People? Meaning normal people?
Raleigh	*Yes.*
Jack	No.
Raleigh	*Did your wives know?*
Jack	My ex-wife did.
Raleigh	*So you had children while you were married to her?*
Jack	That's how I knew I wasn't the cause.
Raleigh	*So that was proof to you?*
Jack	Yes.
Raleigh	*Did you care for your other children?*
Jack	Sure, I care for all kids.
Raleigh	*Did you provide specially?*
Jack	Yes! Yes!
Raleigh	*Did you do it in person, or did you have someone do it for you?*
Jack	I'm not sure I understand.
Raleigh	*Did these children know you were their father?*
Jack	No.
Raleigh	*So they never met you?*
Jack	When they were young.
Raleigh	*Not later on when they would remember you?*
Jack	I wasn't around.
Raleigh	*Were these women from other countries or French?*
Jack	Other country. Just one.
Raleigh	*You only had one child? Is that right?*
Jack	Yes.
Raleigh	*What country was that?*
Jack	Poland.
Raleigh	*Was she pretty?*
Jack	Yes.

Raleigh	*Did you speak the language?*
Jack	No.
Raleigh	*So how did you and this woman get together then?*
Jack	She came to me.
Raleigh	*Could she speak French?*
Jack	A little.
Raleigh	*So I take it she offered herself to you. Is that right?* *[No answer.]* *What did she come for?*
Jack	To take care of me.
Raleigh	*Was this like a servant?*
Jack	No! No!
Raleigh	*Was she royalty? Better yet, just tell me how this came about. You are in Poland, correct?*
Jack	Yes.
Raleigh	*Was it on peaceful terms or war?*
Jack	Peaceful? No.
Raleigh	*So it was war times, or headed toward war?*
Jack	Yes.
Raleigh	*What was your purpose there? Was it to wage war, or try to talk it over so you don't have to?*
Jack	To talk this time.
Raleigh	*So did the leaders arrange this woman to come to you?*
Jack	No! No!
Raleigh	*Okay, she came to serve you, and she was from Poland.*
Jack	Yes.
Raleigh	*She had nothing to do with the war talks?*
Jack	No. They offered me to stay at their house.
Raleigh	*Did she know who you were?*
Jack	Yes.
Raleigh	*Was she afraid of you?*
Jack	No. No.

Raleigh	*Was she married?*
Jack	Yes.
Raleigh	*Where was the husband?*
Jack	He's there.
Raleigh	*So did the husband offer to take care of you?*
Jack	Yes.
Raleigh	*Is that a custom there? To sleep with the husband's wife?*
Jack	Umm, umm. [Small chuckle.]
Raleigh	*Did you feel awkward about that?*
Jack	Yes.
Raleigh	*What did you think about that? Did the husband just say, "Here, sleep with my wife"?*
Jack	No, he never said anything. No, he's older, much older.
Raleigh	*What did she say? I mean, did you question it since the husband was right there?*
Jack	Sure.
Raleigh	*What did she say?*
Jack	That he wants me to be happy.
Raleigh	*Did she have children of her own at that time?*
Jack	No.
Raleigh	*Did the husband raise the child like it was his own?*
Jack	Yes! Yes!
Raleigh	*How did you know you had a child from her? You surely didn't stay nine months with her, did you?*
Jack	No.
Raleigh	*So how did you know?*
Jack	By courier.
Raleigh	*She sent you a message?*
Jack	Yes.
Raleigh	*What did you think about that?*
Jack	I was happy.

Raleigh	*Did you provide money, then, to care for the child?*
Jack	There was no need, but yes, yes, I did.
Raleigh	*Did you tell your wife at that time? Before you divorced her?*
Jack	Yes.
Raleigh	*What did she say?*
Jack	She was upset.
Raleigh	*Was this the only time that this had happened? Similar circumstances? Or did you have a lot of women?*
Jack	No, could have though.
Raleigh	*Could have, but didn't take the opportunity?*
Jack	Yes.
Raleigh	*Did you feel that was a mistake?*
Jack	Yes.
Raleigh	*Because you cared that much about the wife?*
Jack	Yes, and that is what started the divorce.
Raleigh	*You knew you could have kids and she couldn't.*
Jack	Yes.
Raleigh	*Were you married a long time?*
Jack	Pretty long, yes.
Raleigh	*How long is pretty long?*
Jack	A little over 14 years.
Raleigh	*Let's go, now, a little back into your childhood. It will be happy times of your childhood. Let's go to when you were in your 20s. What do you see?*
Jack	Sand.
Raleigh	*What about the sand?*
Jack	Uh, it's sand.
Raleigh	*Where are you at?*
Jack	Egypt.
Raleigh	*What do you think of Egypt?*
Jack	I like it.

Raleigh	*In what way?*
Jack	A lot of tradition. A lot of history.
Raleigh	*Let me ask this: it has been stated that your soldiers were the ones who shot the nose off the Sphinx with cannon fire.*
Jack	No.
Raleigh	*What would you have said if someone would have done that?*
Jack	Umm, I don't understand.
Raleigh	*Did you respect what you were seeing?*
Jack	Yes!
Raleigh	*So this would have made you angry?*
Jack	Yes! Yes!
Raleigh	*Did you allow any of your soldiers to pillage, or plunder, or disfigure anything there?*
Jack	No! My soldiers did nothing unless I told them to do or not to do.
Raleigh	*Okay.*
Jack	They didn't just run as they seen fit.
Raleigh	*Why did you go to Egypt?*
Jack	To learn.
Raleigh	*What did you want to learn?*
Jack	More about where we come from.
Raleigh	*Let's go to your most amazing discovery. What did you discover? Anything unusual?*
Jack	Yes, that there is a strange force, a strange power.
Raleigh	*What makes you think that there is such a force?*
Jack	You can sense it. You can feel it like a … umm ….
Raleigh	*Did you see the pyramids?*
Jack	Yes, yes.
Raleigh	*Who do you feel built the pyramids?*
Jack	Not the people living there!

Raleigh	*What do you feel about the people living there?*
Jack	Very little minds, very primitive, very simple.
Raleigh	*Okay, but you feel the pyramids quite complex?*
Jack	Yes, yes, yes, yes!
Raleigh	*You said you were looking to find where we came from. What did you find?*
Jack	It wasn't the beginnings that we have been told.
Raleigh	*The beginnings of what?*
Jack	The stories we are told. After being there, what we are being told doesn't make sense.
Raleigh	*You are talking about what you are told in France; and after being there, it doesn't make sense?*
Jack	Yes, yes.
Raleigh	*As Emperor, what was the proudest moment of your life? And then we will go to the negative side.*
Jack	Freeing people from their kings that control them.
Raleigh	*You didn't like kings at all, did you?*
Jack	No.
Raleigh	*No respect for a king at all?*
Jack	No, no, none at all.
Raleigh	*Is this the reason you didn't care for England? Because of kings and queens?*
Jack	They didn't like me!
Raleigh	*But you liked freeing people from kings and queens?*
Jack	That's why they didn't like me!
Raleigh	*That stands to reason why history portrays you in this way. What was your most disappointing time?*
Jack	As Emperor?
Raleigh	*Yes.*
Jack	Giving France back to a king.
Raleigh	*You loved France, didn't you?*
Jack	Yes, all of Europe.

Raleigh	*Let's go back into your past a little bit. Why did you dislike kings so much? What was it about a king that you didn't like? It appears you felt this way for some time. Was it before you were an emperor?*
Jack	No!
Raleigh	*No? So when did this feeling begin?*
Jack	Once I started learning the truth.
Raleigh	*Okay, enough of that. Let's go through some happy memories of your childhood. Did you have brothers or sisters?*
Jack	Yes.
Raleigh	*Do you like your brothers and sisters?*
Jack	Yes, I love my family.
Raleigh	*What did you like to do with your family for fun?*
Jack	Talk … about anything.
Raleigh	*Talk, okay. What was your mom and dad like?*
Jack	They were good people.
Raleigh	*Average people?*
Jack	My dad was more average, but my mother was very beautiful.
Raleigh	*More so than the other children's mothers?*
Jack	Yes.
Raleigh	*Did they ever tell you that your mother was very pretty?*
Jack	Yes.
Raleigh	*And you agreed?*
Jack	Yes.
Raleigh	*What age are we seeing right now?*
Jack	Ten.
Raleigh	*Who was your best friend around 10?*
Jack	Ciprianni.
Raleigh	*Okay, is this a boy or a girl?*
Jack	A boy. [Small laugh.]

Raleigh	*Okay, that's a tough name. What do you and Ciprianni like to do?*
Jack	Play war.
Raleigh	*Who is the good guy, and who is the bad guy?*
Jack	We are both the good guys.
Raleigh	*Let's come up in time to the time you lost your life. You know this has already happened, don't you?*
Jack	Yes, I was sick.
Raleigh	*Okay, what part of you was sick?*
Jack	My body.
Raleigh	*All of you, then?*
Jack	Yes.
Raleigh	*Fever?*
Jack	Yes.
Raleigh	*One question before we go any further: were you ever wounded in battle?*
Jack	Very minor.
Raleigh	*I have one more question.*
Jack	Okay.
Raleigh	*In all paintings of you, your hand is inside your jacket. Why?*
Jack	Ha-ha, because it was comfortable.
Raleigh	*There has been controversy about the reason for this for years and years and years, that there was something wrong with your hand.*
Jack	No, there was nothing wrong.
Raleigh	*Did this make you look more authoritative, in this posture?*
Jack	No, I didn't need that.
Raleigh	*Is this something you did all your life?*
Jack	Yes.
Raleigh	*Did you have pockets?*

Jack	Sloppy to have hands in your pockets.
Raleigh	*Just curious, and you are the only man who can answer the questions. Let's come up in time. You were sick, correct?*
Jack	Yes.
Raleigh	*Was there anyone with you?*
Jack	Yes, a lot of people.
Raleigh	*Did your son live to see this day? Is he with you?*
Jack	No, no.
Raleigh	*Was he alive?*
Jack	Yes.
Raleigh	*You were in exile, correct?*
Jack	Yes.
Raleigh	*Was your family in exile as well?*
Jack	No.
Raleigh	*So this is why your son wasn't with you?*
Jack	Yes.
Raleigh	*Were you close to your son emotionally?*
Jack	Yes, I cared for my son.
Raleigh	*Did he care for you?*
Jack	He didn't really know me.
Raleigh	*Let's continue on. You had a fever, correct?*
Jack	Yes.
Raleigh	*Did you die this day?*
Jack	Yes.
Raleigh	*Were there people there, and were they mourning you?*
Jack	Some.
Raleigh	*These were friends with you?*
Jack	Not friends, no, no.
Raleigh	*Who was with you, then?*
Jack	People of my court.
Raleigh	*These were people who were exiled with you?*

Jack	Yes.
Raleigh	*Was a priest there since you were Catholic?*
Jack	No, not when I died, no.
Raleigh	*So you didn't get your last rites?*
Jack	Yes, yes, I did, just not this day.
Raleigh	*Did you think that was important?*
Jack	Not really.
Raleigh	*We are now speaking in terms of your religious values in your life. When you were Emperor, you took the crown. You took the crown away and placed it on your own head. Why did you do this?*
Jack	Because I am not their servant!
Raleigh	*Did you think about doing this, or was it a spur-of-the-moment thing? Had you thought about it?*
Jack	No.
Raleigh	*Okay, you have passed on. What happened to you next?*
Jack	The white.
Raleigh	*Did you stay with your body?*
Jack	Yes.
Raleigh	*For how long?*
Jack	I don't know.
Raleigh	*Did you see your own funeral?*
Jack	Yes.
Raleigh	*Were you buried with honors?*
Jack	What do you mean?
Raleigh	*Were you buried as a great hero?*
Jack	By the British?
Raleigh	*Oh, the British buried you?*
Jack	Yes.
Raleigh	*Were you in Elba when you died?*
Jack	No.
Raleigh	*Where were you?*

Jack	Some nasty rock, St. Helena.
Raleigh	*St. Helena? Like some little island?*
Jack	Yes.
Raleigh	*Where is that at?*
Jack	I … I don't know. We were on board ship for a very, very long time.
Raleigh	*Were they holding you like a prisoner?*
Jack	No, I got along with them.
Raleigh	*So you weren't being treated like a criminal?*
Jack	The officers, no.
Raleigh	*Not the officers, but the men?*
Jack	The men, no.
Raleigh	*So who treated you bad?*
Jack	The British government.
Raleigh	*So, the government sending you to this island is what you are saying was bad?*
Jack	Yes.
Raleigh	*Okay, getting back to your burial, you were given a proper burial?*
Jack	Yes.
Raleigh	*Not just stuck in a hole and forgotten?*
Jack	No.
Raleigh	*It wasn't a big, fancy burial either?*
Jack	No.
Raleigh	*It was fairly quiet.*
Jack	There was people there.
Raleigh	*Friends?*
Jack	No, no friends.
Raleigh	*No family?*
Jack	No.
Raleigh	*People did come though. Where did you go from there? What happened next?*

Jack	Nothing.
Raleigh	*Okay, I know there is a transition of when you left your body to now.*
Jack	I'm still there.
Raleigh	*After you died, who came to meet you?*
Jack	When after I died?
Raleigh	*At any point after you died. Someone came to meet you, didn't they?*
Jack	I don't see anything.
Raleigh	*Okay, I'll get more specific. What happened after the funeral?*
Jack	Nothing … nothing … I'm still there.
Raleigh	*Were you buried at sea or in the ground?*
Jack	In the ground.
Raleigh	*I know from experience, that at some point in time, God spoke to you. At what point did He speak to you?*
Jack	At what point?
Raleigh	*He came to speak to you, or we wouldn't be talking today. Tell me about that meeting. What happened?*
Jack	He said, "You tried."
Raleigh	*He said, "You tried"? Do you see Him?*
Jack	I know He's near me.
Raleigh	*Okay, say exactly what is being told to you, word for word. Do you understand? What is He saying?*
Jack	He's saying that, "You have tried to help people break away from the …."
Raleigh	*From the what?*
Jack	From whatever is holding them back.
Raleigh	*He is talking to you about your life as Emperor, is that correct?*
Jack	Yes.

Raleigh	*Just say it as He is saying it to you. Do you understand?*
Jack	Yes.
Raleigh	*Just repeat what is being told to you. This is the most important part of the text we are writing down. Also, tell me what you are seeing as well. What do you see?*
Jack	It's a … it's like a … it's just white. All white.
Raleigh	*Are there other people around?*
Jack	No.
Raleigh	*Only you?*
Jack	Yes.
Raleigh	*How are you clothed? Look at yourself.*
Jack	Too bright.
Raleigh	*Okay, that's alright. But it's a bright light, is that correct?*
Jack	Yes.
Raleigh	*Where is God in relation to where you are at?*
Jack	He's everywhere.
Raleigh	*Okay.*
Jack	He's there. He's just there. [Pointing ahead.]
Raleigh	*Do you ever see an image of Him such as a physical appearance?*
Jack	No, it's so bright.
Raleigh	*Now, what did He tell you? He is talking to the one and only Napoleon Bonaparte. Someone, through the course of time, may have gotten a bad rap for how he has been perceived. What is He telling you?*
Jack	He tells me, "You tried to help people. You tried to help people break free from their bondage while losing all that makes you happy. You've done well."
Raleigh	*What else?*
Jack	That's all He said.
Raleigh	*Were you told that we would talk?*

Jack   He said we would meet.

Raleigh   *What did He say? Hopefully, it was good things. Did He tell you why?*

Jack   To learn again.

Raleigh   *To learn again by talking to me?*

Jack   To help to open, yes.

Raleigh   *What did you learn from all of this, or are you to teach me?*

Jack   I don't know at this time.

Raleigh   *But He did say we would meet and that this is a good thing?*

Jack   Yes.

EPISODE 10

◆ On a Beach ◆

AT THIS TIME, I would like to introduce you to Kevin. We have been friends for many years. Kevin has a son and is a single parent. He is a superintendent at a manufacturing plant.

I wanted to include this story, but I didn't think I had a session on tape. Because of our busy schedules, Kevin and I couldn't find time to record one. Much to my surprise, I found a tape that I forgot I had. Not that my memory is that short, but it was included with another session I had recorded at one of my lectures.

Many young men and women are facing the unknown during these times of hatred, fighting, and wars. There are also many confused family members left behind by this mayhem. The story you are about to read hits at the very heart of this issue. It shows the extreme love between a mother and child. It also shows how hard it is to simply let go. To lose a child is one of the hardest things a parent could possibly experience — I know because I've been there. But once the pain has calmed to a mild roar, it is important to open your heart so your loved ones can do what they have to do. Knowing they will be in your arms again someday lessens that pain.

With that in mind, let's begin our next journey.

Raleigh   *We are now going to another time, another place, before you were born. A place you know nothing of. What do you see?*

Kevin	A beach.
Raleigh	*A beach, okay. Tell me about it.*
Kevin	It's not a good place.
Raleigh	*It's not a good place, okay. Where is this beach? Like on a river, a lake, what?*
Kevin	An ocean. Barbed wire.
Raleigh	*Barbed wire? Is that what you said?*
Kevin	Yes.
Raleigh	*Are there people around?*
Kevin	Yes.
Raleigh	*Describe the people around you.*
Kevin	They are all dressed in green.
Raleigh	*Okay, what is the nationality of these people? As you look at them, what do you see? [I notice he is very uncomfortable.] Are you in pain?*
Kevin	Yes.
Raleigh	*Okay, let's just back away from that picture. Okay?*
Kevin	Okay.
Raleigh	*Let's go a little earlier. What do you see?*
Kevin	A boat.
Raleigh	*Alright, the next thing I want you to do is to describe yourself.*
Kevin	I'm scared.
Raleigh	*Okay, you're scared, just take it easy. How old are you?*
Kevin	Seventeen.
Raleigh	*Are you afraid of me?*
Kevin	No.
Raleigh	*So you trust me?*
Kevin	Yes.
Raleigh	*Okay, I will take the pain from you, so let's just talk back and forth. Let's look at a more pleasant time in your life when you were happy. What do you see?*

Kevin	My birthday.
Raleigh	*Your birthday? How old are you?*
Kevin	Eleven.
Raleigh	*Tell me what you look like.*
Kevin	Short, black hair.
Raleigh	*Okay. Short, black hair.*
Kevin	I'm a fat boy.
Raleigh	*Ha-ha. So you are a fat boy!*
Kevin	Yes. I have cake on my face.
Raleigh	*You have cake on your face?*
Kevin	It's chocolate with white frosting and my mom's wiping it off.
Raleigh	*Is this a pretty good day?*
Kevin	Yes, a good day.
Raleigh	*Tell me what your name is. What's your name?*
Kevin	Joseph.
Raleigh	*Joseph? Okay, Joseph, I want you to stay right where you are. It's your birthday. Okay?*
Kevin	Yes.
Raleigh	*I want you to enjoy where you are; after all, it's your birthday. Understand?*
Kevin	Yes.
Raleigh	*You will remain at this party until I speak directly to you again. Do you understand?*
Kevin	Yes.
Raleigh	*[This is being done in front of a group of people during one of my many lectures and demonstrations. Kevin, or at this time Joseph, is now unaware of the present time, so I am able to address the people who have come to watch.]*
	If you have been listening, his name in a previous life is Joseph. As you can see, we are now going down

through his life in the same fashion that we did for Kevin. As his story unfolds, we are seeing more than likely a soldier or a captive somewhere. We don't know exactly what, yet. There are times when I take people back and it is at the time of their death where we cross first. This is one of the most, I don't know if tragic is the proper term, but at least the most memorable times of life. This is why we try to move off the subject as quickly as possible so I can approach the issue in a more controlled condition.

When it comes time for the subject to experience his or her death, I do not let the person relive the pain. At this point, they merely describe to us what is taking place and what happened. There is no reason to make the person uncomfortable, so even going through the process of death can be an interesting experience. Remember, I would like these people to come back to help me look for missing children, future events, and whatever else we are working on. If this was a horrible experience, I would doubt Kevin would be here. And more than likely you wouldn't be watching, hoping there is time for at least one more session.

As we go further in Joseph's life, we should learn more about him. Did he have a family? Does he have brothers or sisters? We will go through the different stages of his life, whether is was short or long, and then travel on past his death. You will then be able to see what really happens after you die. You will see what heaven is like and why Joseph is here for Kevin.

Question [From member of audience.] Can you find the exact time he died or just the why?

Raleigh *It all depends on how I wish to approach it. We are going through Joseph's life in the same manner that we did Kevin's. Try to imagine that he is traveling in a time machine through history and that we can stop and look around at any time of that person's life. To them, all the sights, sounds, smells, etcetera are as real to them as we are in this room at this minute in time. Once again, however, because I wish this to be a pleasurable as well as an incredible voyage, I try to stick to a positive theme of one's life. Now, let's get back to going through Joseph's life. We may stop again for more questions later on.*

Okay, Joseph.

Kevin Yes?

Raleigh *You are still at the party, correct?*

Kevin Yes.

Raleigh *What did you get for presents that day?*

Kevin Toy soldiers, little soldiers in a box. They're fun!

Raleigh *They're fun, okay. You're 11?*

Kevin Yes.

Raleigh *What is ... what day is your birthday?*

Kevin I'm not sure.

Raleigh *What year is it now? Look at the calendar. Is there one close to where you are at?*

Kevin 1910?

Raleigh *1910. Okay, trust it. Is your whole family with you?*

Kevin Just my sister and my mom.

Raleigh *Okay, your sister and your mom.*

Kevin And my grandpa!

Raleigh *Where is your dad?*

Kevin My dad's dead.

Raleigh	*I'm sorry, but you are still having fun this day, aren't you?*
Kevin	Yes.
Raleigh	*Joseph, what is your last name?*
Kevin	Dugan. [Slightly inaudible.]
Raleigh	*Duncan?*
Kevin	Dugan! D-U-G-A-N!
Raleigh	*Do you know what town you live in?*
Kevin	That's too hard.
Raleigh	*Okay, I won't mess with you on your birthday. Let's now go to a happy time when you are 15. It's a happy time. What do you see?*
Kevin	I got a girl!
Raleigh	*You got a girl? What does she look like?*
Kevin	Long blonde hair. Her breasts, they … they just stick out.
Raleigh	*I take it they stick out pretty good?*
Kevin	Oh, yeah! [Great big smile.]
Raleigh	*Have you known her for some time?*
Kevin	I went to school with her.
Raleigh	*She went to school with you. Is she the same age as you?*
Kevin	A year younger.
Raleigh	*Where did you go to school?*
Kevin	Madison Junior High.
Raleigh	*What town is this?*
Kevin	Shreveport.
Raleigh	*Shreveport, Louisiana?*
Kevin	Yes.
Raleigh	*Tell me a little bit about your girlfriend. Why is she such a special girl?*
Kevin	Well, you know, talking to her. [Big smile.]
Raleigh	*Just talking to her?*

Kevin	Well, there's other things.
Raleigh	*Ha-ha. Have you been going with her for some time?*
Kevin	Yes.
Raleigh	*What do you like the best about her?*
Kevin	The way she laughs, and she thinks I'm funny.
Raleigh	*Are you funny?*
Kevin	I ... I hope so.
Raleigh	*You hope so. Well, it seems like you have a pretty good personality. What does she call you?*
Kevin	Sugar Lips. [Red-faced.]
Raleigh	*Sugar Lips! What do you call her?*
Kevin	Pertie Gertie.
Raleigh	*Pertie Gertie? How did you come up with Pertie Gertie?*
Kevin	It was her breasts.
Raleigh	*Ha-ha, I take it they were pretty well endowed.*
Kevin	[A nod of the head and Cheshire Cat smile.]
Raleigh	*Is she a thin girl?*
Kevin	A little heavier than I am.
Raleigh	*So you are still heavy-set?*
Kevin	Yes.
Raleigh	*What is Gertrude's full name? Gertrude what?*
Kevin	Gertrude Ann Walker.
Raleigh	*Gertrude Ann Walker, okay. [At this point Kevin starts to become a little uncomfortable again.] Okay, let's come up to a time that is a little more pleasant. Do you understand? A time that's a little more pleasant.*
Kevin	Yes.
Raleigh	*How old are you now?*
Kevin	... My time with Gertrude ....

Raleigh	*The questions I am now about to ask may sound very strange to you, but I think by now you are starting to feel that these events have already happened. You are beginning to understand that, aren't you?*
Kevin	Yes.
Raleigh	*Do you trust what I am telling you?*
Kevin	Yes.
Raleigh	*You know now that we are traveling through your life through time, don't you?*
Kevin	Yes.
Raleigh	*The questions I am about to ask you are not intended to frighten you for they have already happened; they have already passed. Do you understand that?*
Kevin	Yes.
Raleigh	*So you trust what I am telling you?*
Kevin	Yes.
Raleigh	*I want you to go ahead in time now, and I am going to ask you a series of questions. Did you live to see age 25?*
Kevin	No.
Raleigh	*No. So you know now time has passed, don't you?*
Kevin	Yes.
Raleigh	*Just listen carefully as I speak. We have learned a great deal about you, and we want to know all there is to know about your life. Okay?*
Kevin	Yes.
Raleigh	*Did you see age 20?*
Kevin	No.
Raleigh	*Did you see age 19?*
Kevin	No.
Raleigh	*Did you see age 18?*
Kevin	No.

Raleigh	*Okay, we knew you saw age 17, so I want you to relax, and we are going to talk about age 17. Okay?*
Kevin	Yes.
Raleigh	*There is no doubt you were somewhere at war. Is that correct?*
Kevin	Yes.
Raleigh	*Did you join the Service?*
Kevin	Yes.
Raleigh	*What did you do?*
Kevin	The Marines.
Raleigh	*The Marines. How old were you when you joined them?*
Kevin	Sixteen.
Raleigh	*You were 16, okay. Why did you join?*
Kevin	I wanted my mom to be proud of me.
Raleigh	*To make your mom proud of you. You said earlier that your father was dead. Was he a soldier?*
Kevin	She never talked about it.
Raleigh	*Okay, did your mom want you to join the military?*
Kevin	It was my decision. I thought it was the right thing to do.
Raleigh	*Where were you shipped to when you were age 17? [Kevin is now very uneasy and starting to move about.] What is the matter?*
Kevin	The pain!
Raleigh	*Okay, let me remove the pain. You are not reliving. You are only describing the events taking place. You are not reliving, you are not there anymore. These events have already happened. Whatever you went through has already happened. You are only telling about it. Understand?*
Kevin	[Much calmer.] Yes.
Raleigh	*Where were you sent to?*

Kevin	We were not told.
Raleigh	*You didn't even know?*
Kevin	No. [Very upset.] We asked, but no answer. What is wrong … this can't be.
Raleigh	*Did you feel you made a mistake?*
Kevin	I can't accept it.
Raleigh	*You didn't accept it at the time?*
Kevin	No.
Raleigh	*So you can't accept it now?*
Kevin	No.
Raleigh	*We won't dwell a great deal on this, other than the fact you were probably dropped on some beach and there was a battle going on. Correct?*
Kevin	Yes.
Raleigh	*Was this when you died?*
Kevin	Not yet.
Raleigh	*Was it shortly after you saw these people around you that you died?*
Kevin	Yes.
Raleigh	*How did you die?*
Kevin	I was shot.
Raleigh	*Okay.*
Kevin	Twice.
Raleigh	*Were you sent home?*
Kevin	Yes.
Raleigh	*Did you travel with your body?*
Kevin	Yes … kind of. I followed it.
Raleigh	*You followed it?*
Kevin	Yes.
Raleigh	*Did you feel your soul leave your body?*
Kevin	Yes.

Raleigh	*Did you leave the battle scene immediately, or did you stay with your body?*
Kevin	I stayed until I was found.
Raleigh	*Okay.*
Kevin	I couldn't understand.
Raleigh	*You couldn't understand what happened?*
Kevin	No.
Raleigh	*Okay. You followed your family home?*
Kevin	Yes.
Raleigh	*Did you see your family?*
Kevin	"I'm so sorry, Mom! I'm so sorry, Mom!"
Raleigh	*Did you try to tell her that?*
Kevin	Yes.
Raleigh	*How did you try to do that?*
Kevin	I can see her, but why can't she see me?
Raleigh	*Okay, what did you do next after all the funeral and everything is over? What happened?*
Kevin	I felt light.
Raleigh	*You felt light. What event took place next which made it possible for you to go on?*
Kevin	Mom let go.
Raleigh	*Did you stay with her for a long time?*
Kevin	She couldn't accept what had happened.
Raleigh	*So what was the turning point for her?*
Kevin	She finally cried.
Raleigh	*She cried?*
Kevin	She cried and let me go.
Raleigh	*She cried and let you go. And when you left, where did you go then?*
Kevin	I'm not sure, but it was peaceful.
Raleigh	*It was peaceful. Let's go now to where you actually saw someone. Who did you see?*

Kevin	I met my father. I had never seen my father.
Raleigh	*You met your father? How is he dressed?*
Kevin	Long coat and tails, a fancy hat. He has a long handlebar mustache.
Raleigh	*Did he talk to you?*
Kevin	He told me that I had a lot to do and that he was my father.
Raleigh	*Did he take you to God?*
Kevin	It's like a waiting area.
Raleigh	*Like a waiting room? Were there … other people there?*
Kevin	Lots, lots.
Raleigh	*Anybody we know?*
Kevin	No.
Raleigh	*How are you dressed?*
Kevin	I'm still wearing what I got shot in.
Raleigh	*Okay, still the uniform, but at peace. Who now came and got you? How are these people dressed?*
Kevin	Like how my mom would dress.
Raleigh	*How would that be like?*
Kevin	Long dress, well, like an old lady.
Raleigh	*Okay, where were you taken then?*
Kevin	Small room, white all around.
Raleigh	*Let's come ahead to where you meet God.*
Kevin	I never made it there.
Raleigh	*Who finally came and got you?*
Kevin	There was something left undone.
Raleigh	*Is this what you were told?*
Kevin	Yes.
Raleigh	*Let's come to the point where you were told that there was something left undone, and say it word for word as you hear it.*

Kevin	"It is not yet your time, for you still have things to do. You have been taken before your time, so you will not see Me — the Face of God." I asked what that is. All there was is silence.
Raleigh	*Were you told we would meet today?*
Kevin	Yes.
Raleigh	*You were? Who told you? And what were you told?*
Kevin	That we would talk and that this would be the first step for me to enter the light.
Raleigh	*Okay. What kind of things are you being told about?*
Kevin	Lots, that I must help.
Raleigh	*What were you told when you were taken to Kevin?*
Kevin	That he was a sad soul and needed help.
Raleigh	*Have you helped him?*
Kevin	I've tried.
Raleigh	*It does appear to me that you have the personality to cheer him up. In regard to our reading today, were you given any reason why we would meet?*
Kevin	To help Kevin.

I have been researching this story. Between the years of 1916 and 1917, there were 19 Marines killed in battle on the island of Haiti and another 17 Marines killed in battle on the island of the Dominican Republic. Was young Joseph Dugan one of those? I have not yet been able to find out, but my personal feelings tell me yes. This story shows you can die before your expected time and you may not have finished everything on earth that needed to be accomplished. Joseph is not being punished for this, and God gives him the opportunity to achieve a higher level. I would not be surprised one bit if, the next time I talk to Joseph, his Marine greens have been replaced by a white robe.

EPISODE 11

◆ A Field of Wildflowers ◆

I MET KATHY several years ago at a psychic fair where I was giving a seminar. She is married and has two grown children. Recently she became a master of Reiki. This is not an easy thing to do, and it requires great dedication. Even so, there has never been a time when I have asked for assistance on a case — missing person or otherwise — that she has refused me.

We will now continue our journey through time with her helper, Jenna.

Raleigh	*We are now going to another time, another place you know nothing of. What do you see? What is the first thing that comes to mind?*
Kathy	Fields.
Raleigh	*What about the fields? What time of the year is it?*
Kathy	Spring.
Raleigh	*Then everything is ... okay .... What kind of day is it?*
Kathy	Sunny day.
Raleigh	*And where are you at?*
Kathy	I'm in some wildflowers.
Raleigh	*What color are they?*
Kathy	Yellow and white.
Raleigh	*Yellow and white, okay. What are you doing this day?*
Kathy	I'm picking some flowers for a nosegay.
Raleigh	*For a what?*

Kathy   Yes, they are a tiny bouquet. They call them a nosegay.

Raleigh   *A nosegay, okay.*

Kathy   Hmm ....

Raleigh   *What's the matter?*

Kathy   It's almost May.

Raleigh   *Almost May?*

Kathy   Yes, the flowers are for May Day.

Raleigh   *Do you like May Day?*

Kathy   Yes, it is a big celebration.

Raleigh   *What do you look like?*

Kathy   Long hair.

Raleigh   *Long hair. What color?*

Kathy   Hmm. Red.

Raleigh   *Red. How old are you?*

Kathy   Seventeen.

Raleigh   *Are you tall, thin, short, what?*

Kathy   I'm not tall, but I'm also not short. I guess you could call it average height.

Raleigh   *Average height. And how are you dressed?*

Kathy   Blue skirt with a white blouse. I ... I have a black shawl.

Raleigh   *A black shawl?*

Kathy   Uh-huh. It seems a little bit chilly.

Raleigh   *Okay, what is your name?*

Kathy   Jenna Marie.

Raleigh   *Is that your ... Jenna Marie?*

Kathy   Uh-huh.

Raleigh   *Jenna Marie what? What is your last name?*

Kathy   It will be McLaughlin. I'm getting married in a few days.

Raleigh   *That's a few days away. What is it now?*

Kathy	Monahan, but it sounds funny somehow.
Raleigh	*Why's that?*
Kathy	My new name starts with an "M" also.
Raleigh	*Ha-ha.*
Kathy	I guess it just dawned on ....
Raleigh	*It was Monahan, correct?*
Kathy	Uh-huh.
Raleigh	*What is your husband-to-be's name, his first name?*
Kathy	Connor.
Raleigh	*Connor McLaughlin? Is that right?*
Kathy	Uh-huh, I call him Conn.
Raleigh	*And you are 17. Alright, what day are you going to get married on?*
Kathy	First of June.
Raleigh	*First of June, okay. Will it be a big wedding?*
Kathy	No, not very big. We don't have a lot of money, so it will have to be small.
Raleigh	*Okay, where are you from?*
Kathy	Outside of Dublin, on the outskirts.
Raleigh	*Do you live in town, on a farm, or what?*
Kathy	On a farm.
Raleigh	*Do you have brothers and sisters?*
Kathy	I have two brothers.
Raleigh	*What are their names? Do they live there at the farm?*
Kathy	Sean is the oldest. And John.
Raleigh	*Okay, are they nice?*
Kathy	Yes, as brothers go.
Raleigh	*Ha-ha. What do you like the best about them?*
Kathy	Hmm, I can talk to them.
Raleigh	*What don't you like about them?*
Kathy	They have a tendency to be bossy.
Raleigh	*A tendency to be bossy? And you don't like that?*

Kathy	No, I have a mind of my own.
Raleigh	*Okay, they are both older, is that right?*
Kathy	Uh-huh.
Raleigh	*You have no sisters?*
Kathy	One, but she died.
Raleigh	*As an infant?*
Kathy	No, as a little girl.
Raleigh	*As a little girl? How old?*
Kathy	She was four.
Raleigh	*And what did she die from?*
Kathy	A lung ailment.
Raleigh	*What was her name?*
Kathy	Bridget.
Raleigh	*Bridget, okay. Let's go to your wedding day. Okay, what year is this right now?*
Kathy	1804.
Raleigh	*1804, okay.*
Kathy	That's the numbers I see.
Raleigh	*Okay, it's now your wedding day. Is it in a church?*
Kathy	It's in the rectory.
Raleigh	*The rectory? Is that part of the church?*
Kathy	It's a small side chapel.
Raleigh	*A small side chapel? Why not the main chapel?*
Kathy	It was prettier.
Raleigh	*It was prettier. Was this your choice?*
Kathy	Yes.
Raleigh	*How are you dressed?*
Kathy	White linen. Couldn't afford the silk. My mother made the dress.
Raleigh	*Was it pretty?*
Kathy	Uh-huh, I think so.
Raleigh	*How is Conner dressed?*

Kathy	A shirtwaist.
Raleigh	*It goes around the waist?*
Kathy	Yes, it just goes down to around the waist, not like a full shirt.
Raleigh	*But he does have a full shirt on as well?*
Kathy	Umm, yes.
Raleigh	*As well as this vest called a shirtwaist?*
Kathy	That's what I see.
Raleigh	*You are going to marry a man this day. Why? What makes him so special that this is the one you wanted to marry?*
Kathy	I don't know. It just happened. He's quite the handsome man.
Raleigh	*Okay, is he older or about the same age?*
Kathy	He's 20.
Raleigh	*Has he had other girlfriends? Other than you?*
Kathy	He says he hasn't, but they all tell you that, don't you know?
Raleigh	*Ha-ha. They all tell you that, okay.*
Kathy	Living in a small place, you know who the others were.
Raleigh	*Okay, so you knew! So it didn't bother you much that he told you otherwise?*
Kathy	No, he chose me. That's all that matters.
Raleigh	*Okay, you said, "I do." Are you happy?*
Kathy	Uh-huh, extremely.
Raleigh	*Extremely, okay. Did you go anywhere for a honeymoon?*
Kathy	No.
Raleigh	*Where do you go after you get married in 1804, right after a wedding?*
Kathy	To your new house!

Raleigh *To your new house, okay. Did you have parties or anything?*

Kathy You know how the Irish drink, of course they partied as long as they could.

Raleigh *They partied as long as they could. Did they get drunk?*

Kathy Hmm … tipsy, maybe.

Raleigh *Did you drink?*

Kathy Some. Not too much.

Raleigh *You don't drink too much?*

Kathy No, don't really care for it.

Raleigh *Okay. Did you have special food for the occasion?*

Kathy Nothing out of the ordinary you would have for the day — potatoes, carrots — Mom made her best bread.

Raleigh *Did you go to your new house?*

Kathy Conner had built the new house a few years ahead. He planned ahead. He wanted to have it done, so that when we got married we could move right into it, and not have to stay with the family.

Raleigh *What does Conn do?*

Kathy He is a smithy.

Raleigh *Oh, hopefully being a smithy pays better than the farm, doesn't it?*

Kathy Not a lot, but he has more money than my family.

Raleigh *Where did he learn to be a smithy?*

Kathy From his dad.

Raleigh *His dad?*

Kathy Uh-huh.

Raleigh *The trade was passed down through the family?*

Kathy That's what you are taught. Whatever your father did.

Raleigh *Okay, you started your new life together. Was it good?*

Kathy Hmm, yes.

Raleigh	*Better than what you had before?*
Kathy	I missed my family, but they live just down the road so it won't be so bad.
Raleigh	*Okay, let's go up in time a little bit. You're 17 now, so let's go up a little bit to when you were 25, okay? What's life like now at 25?*
Kathy	Just like it was before, except now I'm more settled in. I have children.
Raleigh	*You have children now? How old were you when you had your first one?*
Kathy	I was 19. I didn't have children right away.
Raleigh	*What was your first child?*
Kathy	A son. We named him John.
Raleigh	*How many children did you have?*
Kathy	I had three living, but I lost a fourth one.
Raleigh	*What was your second child?*
Kathy	Another boy. We named him Ian.
Raleigh	*How old were you?*
Kathy	I was 21.
Raleigh	*What do you think about childbirth?*
Kathy	They sure don't tell you about it. It's a lot of work.
Raleigh	*What was your last child?*
Kathy	A girl. We named her Mary.
Raleigh	*Did you have a child you had a closer relation to?*
Kathy	Yes, probably Ian, because he was born in winter and I got to spend more time with him.
Raleigh	*Was a doctor present?*
Kathy	There was a midwife. She did all the doctoring.
Raleigh	*How old were you with the last child?*
Kathy	I just turned 25.
Raleigh	*Is there anything you would like to tell about the children?*

Kathy   They were good children. They had to work hard.

Raleigh   *Did you ever learn to read and write?*

Kathy   Uh-huh.

Raleigh   *You felt that was important?*

Kathy   Uh-huh, it could take me places I could never go.

Raleigh   *What was your favorite book that you ever read?*

Kathy   It was quite naughty.

Raleigh   *Ha-ha. And where did you get that?*

Kathy   A friend loaned it to me.

Raleigh   *It was pretty risqué?*

Kathy   Oh, yes, I read the whole book, you see, because in the Holy Book there wasn't much to read.

Raleigh   *What part of the Holy Book did you like the most?*

Kathy   Nothing really, it was just what you were supposed to read.

Raleigh   *What do you like to do?*

Kathy   I like baking bread and pies.

Raleigh   *Are you baking right now?*

Kathy   Uh-huh, a blackberry pie.

Raleigh   *Do you have your own oven?*

Kathy   It's built into the house. All the houses do.

Raleigh   *Oh, so it's like a fireplace?*

Kathy   No, attached to the fireplace.

Raleigh   *Oh, okay. Please describe what your home is made out of.*

Kathy   It's called wattle. It was made of grass and mud.

Raleigh   *Wattle? Made like a brick?*

Kathy   Uh-huh.

Raleigh   *What about when it rains? Wouldn't it wash the wattle away?*

Kathy   No, because you would put the whitewash on it.

Raleigh   *That would keep it from washing away?*

Kathy	Well, it never did.
Raleigh	*How many rooms did it have?*
Kathy	Living room, short room to store fuel, and a loft upstairs.
Raleigh	*A fairly good-sized house then?*
Kathy	Sometimes I wished it would be a little larger.
Raleigh	*What was the roof made of?*
Kathy	It … thatch … made of grass.
Raleigh	*Wouldn't this let the rain … to come in?*
Kathy	It was done in layers in such a way as to keep the rain out. Oh, yes, there were times where parts may leak, but you could repair it sections at a time.
Raleigh	*Was your house warm with only one fireplace?*
Kathy	There was a small fireplace in the corner of the room if you wanted, but you didn't have to.
Raleigh	*Okay, what kind of a floor did you have?*
Kathy	He put wood down.
Raleigh	*Okay, he put wood down.*
Kathy	Before, we had dirt. It was my idea for the floor. It would be much nicer than walking around in dirt all of the time. I had seen places that had wood floors.
Raleigh	*So wood floors were a little uncommon?*
Kathy	Uh-huh. My family had dirt, but they put rugs to walk on. The rugs only got dirtier.
Raleigh	*Okay, we are going to the time you died. What was happening that day?*
Kathy	Umm, it hurts to breathe.
Raleigh	*The same thing your dad had? [From a previous session.]*
Kathy	No, different.
Raleigh	*What do they call this?*

Kathy	I'm thinking they call it tuberculosis.
Raleigh	*Where did you get that name from?*
Kathy	The doctor.
Raleigh	*The doctor?*
Kathy	Uh-huh, I think that's what he called it.
Raleigh	*Uh-huh.*
Kathy	I was supposed to rest and stay dry.
Raleigh	*Have you had it for some time?*
Kathy	A year. It wasn't so bad in the beginning.
Raleigh	*Do you see 36?*
Kathy	No.
Raleigh	*Let's come back then. How were you on this day?*
Kathy	I was very weak.
Raleigh	*The children were getting older now?*
Kathy	Uh-huh.
Raleigh	*They were still okay?*
Kathy	They were going to be okay. Connor was going to be with them.
Raleigh	*Let's come up to the time where you actually passed on. Okay?*
Kathy	Uh-huh.
Raleigh	*What happened after that? What was it like after you passed on?*
Kathy	The pain was gone.
Raleigh	*At what point did you actually leave your body?*
Kathy	There's Connor and the minister giving me my last rites. It's like I see myself and my family.
Raleigh	*Is this a long time after you died or a short time?*
Kathy	I stayed there for maybe an hour.
Raleigh	*An hour?*
Kathy	Uh-huh. I knew I was supposed to go somewhere, but I didn't want to leave. And then my dad was there.

Raleigh	*Your dad was there?*
Kathy	Yes, and he said it would be all right just to follow him.
Raleigh	*Where did you see your dad at?*
Kathy	He was just over there in the corner.
Raleigh	*Of the room?*
Kathy	Uh-huh.
Raleigh	*Standing, like on the floor?*
Kathy	Yeah, and he told me if I took his hand that I could stand there, too, instead of just afloatin' around. I took his hand, and he said that everybody would be just fine and that everybody just needed to mourn.
Raleigh	*How was he dressed?*
Kathy	They looked like regular clothes.
Raleigh	*Are you still aware of yourself? Like, if you looked down, did you see your hand? Not your body, but when you left your body.*
Kathy	It's like looking through things. You could look, but it wasn't real clear.
Raleigh	*Could you still hear things going on around the room?*
Kathy	Uh-huh.
Raleigh	*Did you leave with your father?*
Kathy	Uh-huh.
Raleigh	*Where did he take you?*
Kathy	Like a beautiful road.
Raleigh	*Where did he finally take you to?*
Kathy	The light at the end.
Raleigh	*Okay, did you see anything else on the sides as you were passing along this road? Or are you looking straight ahead?*
Kathy	I was looking at the light.

Raleigh	*You were looking at the light. Was your father saying anything to you at the time, as you were walking along?*
Kathy	He's telling me everything would be fine, and that he would have to leave for a while, and that I would see him again some other time.
Raleigh	*Okay, did you ask him why he had to leave?*
Kathy	He knew he had other things to do.
Raleigh	*Did he tell you what those things were?*
Kathy	No.
Raleigh	*You didn't know where you were going?*
Kathy	No, but I wasn't afraid.
Raleigh	*At the point at which he left you, look at yourself and tell me how you are clothed.*
Kathy	It appears to be a robe.
Raleigh	*Okay, let's back up a little bit. What color is the robe?*
Kathy	Cream-colored.
Raleigh	*Who gave you this robe?*
Kathy	I was just in the robe. Nobody gave it to me.
Raleigh	*Did you have it when you started … the tunnel?*
Kathy	I didn't have it when I started. It just changed.
Raleigh	*You didn't notice it, and you didn't see anybody?*
Kathy	No, 'cause I was lookin' to the light.
Raleigh	*Now you're in the light. Is that correct?*
Kathy	No, not yet.
Raleigh	*Is there anyone else with you?*
Kathy	I feel people off to my sides.
Raleigh	*Are they looking at you?*
Kathy	I think so.
Raleigh	*Are they men, women, children, or what?*
Kathy	Men.
Raleigh	*Are they in the same color robe as yours?*
Kathy	All different colors.

Raleigh	*What colors do they appear to be?*
Kathy	There are some that appear a light rose color.
Raleigh	*But yours is sort of cream-colored?*
Kathy	Yes, kind of.
Raleigh	*Has anyone spoken to you?*
Kathy	Uh-huh, in front of me.
Raleigh	*What did this person say?*
Kathy	"Come unto Me."
Raleigh	*Can you see this person?*
Kathy	I'm just following this voice. I'm at the bottom of these stairs. There are angels on both sides of the stairs.
Raleigh	*Are these angels men or women?*
Kathy	I think they were both. The light from them, you really couldn't tell if they were male or female.
Raleigh	*Did you hear them speak?*
Kathy	I don't think I really heard their voices. It was their thoughts that they put into my head.
Raleigh	*What did they tell you?*
Kathy	It was kind of like a welcoming committee. They just told me to go up the stairs.
Raleigh	*Were there a lot of stairs?*
Kathy	It didn't seem so at first, but after I think about it, there were a great deal of stairs.
Raleigh	*Were there angels all the way?*
Kathy	Uh-huh, but the angels changed along the way.
Raleigh	*In what way?*
Kathy	The ones toward the top gave off more light.
Raleigh	*So the ones at the top were more powerful?*
Kathy	Uh-huh, it seems so. There were seven of them.
Raleigh	*Did they look different from the others?*
Kathy	They had shields.

Raleigh	*Let's go through one through seven. What do they represent?*
Kathy	The first seems to be the Angel of Peace.
Raleigh	*What was the second one?*
Kathy	It was the Messenger of Hope.
Raleigh	*What is number three?*
Kathy	Ariel is what I'm being told.
Raleigh	*Is this a female?*
Kathy	It's hard to tell. I'm not sure. It's wearing a gold robe. It might be female. I don't know.
Raleigh	*What does this, the next angel, do?*
Kathy	Truth.
Raleigh	*What was number five's job?*
Kathy	A recorder. He writes things in the book.
Raleigh	*Who is the next one?*
Kathy	Michael, the Warrior, the Protector.
Raleigh	*What is the last one?*
Kathy	I don't know. He sits in the chair. I can't see the face. There's this really bright light. He touches my hand.
Raleigh	*He touches your hand?*
Kathy	Uh-huh, and says, "Welcome, My child. Welcome home."

EPISODE 12

◆ Plains and Mountains ◆

IN THE LATE 1970s, Jim and I were co-workers. At that time, he was divorced and had one child. Jim had no previous connection to, or knowledge of, Native-American culture.

This tape is nearly 30 years old, but it is a classic. The transcript begins earlier than the others in order to illustrate the transition from present to past. I hope you enjoy this — it is one of my family's favorites.

Raleigh	*So let's go back now. Let's go back to the day you were born. What's it like the day you were born? You haven't been born yet. In fact, you're still inside your mother. What's it like?*
Jim	It's like … floating … [long pause] … warm.
Raleigh	*Okay, what else?*
Jim	I'm … just … just floating.
Raleigh	*Okay, are you happy?*
Jim	I'm comfortable.
Raleigh	*Okay, is your mother happy?*
Jim	Oh, yes.
Raleigh	*Okay.*
Jim	Talkin' all the time.
Raleigh	*Talkin' all the time. What's she say?*
Jim	There's been talk … she seemed happy … about having another one on the way. She loves me already.

Raleigh	*Okay, does that make you feel good?*
Jim	Yes.
Raleigh	*Okay. What's your father saying?*
Jim	He's happy, but I think he's worried.
Raleigh	*Why is he worried?*
Jim	I don't know.
Raleigh	*Okay, very good. Alright, you are now being born. Coming to the time when you're being born, what's it like?*
Jim	Tight … tight … real tight.
Raleigh	*Okay, alright. You've been born. You are now born. What's it like?*
Jim	All those lights, real bright.
Raleigh	*Can you hear?*
Jim	No.
Raleigh	*Is anybody saying anything?*
Jim	I see a woman.
Raleigh	*Okay, what about her? Who is it?*
Jim	She's there with … with my mother and … and a man.
Raleigh	*Is the man a doctor?*
Jim	Yes. He's … he's cleaning … he's cleaning me.
Raleigh	*Okay. Are you happy?*
Jim	Yes, yes. It feels good.
Raleigh	*Okay.*
Jim	To breathe. It feels good.
Raleigh	*Okay. Has anybody said anything yet?*
Jim	My mother, she's … she's cryin' … she's happy, though.
Raleigh	*Okay.*
Jim	She's … she wants … she wants to know … what I am.

Raleigh	*What did he say?*
Jim	A boy.
Raleigh	*What'd she say?*
Jim	She said, "Tim will be happy."
Raleigh	*Is that your father?*
Jim	Yes.
Raleigh	*Are you the only boy so far?*
Jim	No, John Michael. She said we need to balance … balance it out.
Raleigh	*You've got two boys and two girls?*
Jim	Oh, no. Judy, Terry, Mary, Chris, John Mike, me.
Raleigh	*Three boys and three girls?*
Jim	Four … four girls and me makes two boys.
Raleigh	*Okay, very good, alright. Now I want you to rest … rest … rest. This isn't so hard, is it?*
Jim	No.
Raleigh	*Okay, do you like going down through your life?*
Jim	Some, yes.
Raleigh	*Okay, I can understand that. Have you been seeing things as they are happening? It's as though you are really there?*
Jim	Not all of it's that clear.
Raleigh	*Okay, but when it is?*
Jim	Yes.
Raleigh	*Okay. Alright. Now, I want you to … to listen very carefully. We're going to go back now, to before you're born. Don't let this worry you at all. We're going back, back, back to before you were born. To another time, another place, a place you know nothing about. What do you see? [Long pause.] What comes ….*
Jim	Plains.
Raleigh	*Airplanes?*

Jim	Plains, and mountains beyond.
Raleigh	*Okay. What mountains are these? Where are these mountains located?*
Jim	Here.
Raleigh	*Okay. But what mountain range are they?*
Jim	They call them the Rockies now.
Raleigh	*Okay, what is the year?*
Jim	1811.
Raleigh	*Okay. Can you see yourself yet?*
Jim	Yes.
Raleigh	*Okay, describe yourself.*
Jim	I'm … 18 or 19 years old. Three moons have passed.
Raleigh	*What is your name?*
Jim	Chawtoonaw. [Indian words are spelled phonetically.]
Raleigh	*Okay. You are Indian?*
Jim	Yes.
Raleigh	*Of what tribe?*
Jim	We are Plains.
Raleigh	*The Plains Indian?*
Jim	Yes.
Raleigh	*That's what you call yourself? The Plains Indian? What does the white man call you?*
Jim	That's what he calls us.
Raleigh	*What do you call yourselves? [Long pause.] Do you call yourselves anything?*
Jim	We are small, not many of us.
Raleigh	*Are you a fighting tribe?*
Jim	No.
Raleigh	*What do you do?*
Jim	Hunt … antelope.
Raleigh	*Okay, who is your father?*
Jim	Amontekaw.

Raleigh	*Okay, and who is your mother?*
Jim	She's dead.
Raleigh	*What was her name, though? What did she die from?*
Jim	Fourteen ....
Raleigh	*Fourteen?*
Jim	She took ... she took the spirits.
Raleigh	*Now I want you to rest and think of her. Okay? Rest ... rest and think of your mother. [Turns tape over.] Alright, I'm back. Describe your mother to me. What did she look like?*
Jim	She ... tall. Coal-black hair.
Raleigh	*Is she heavy, thin, what?*
Jim	No, she's thin.
Raleigh	*Is she pretty?*
Jim	Very pretty.
Raleigh	*Okay. How old were you when you last saw your mother?*
Jim	Seven ....
Raleigh	*You were seven?*
Jim	Seventeen summers ... we lived together, before the spirits took her.
Raleigh	*What spirit took her? How many spirits are there? How many do you believe in?*
Jim	Many spirits.
Raleigh	*Who is the ... the main spirit?*
Jim	Oookanaw.
Raleigh	*Oookanaw? What does that stand for?*
Jim	Great One.
Raleigh	*Is he good or bad?*
Jim	He is good if you are good.
Raleigh	*Okay, are you good?*
Jim	Yes.

Raleigh	*Okay. What is your favorite thing in life?*
Jim	Hunting.
Raleigh	*Hunting. And do you have a girlfriend?*
Jim	Oh, no.
Raleigh	*Why?*
Jim	My father will choose my bride.
Raleigh	*Is your father important?*
Jim	He sits on the Council.
Raleigh	*Who is the Chief?*
Jim	Nawaway.
Raleigh	*Nawaway. Okay, is he over the Plains Indians?*
Jim	Our tribe, yes. We are small.
Raleigh	*Okay, how small?*
Jim	Only 40, 50 braves.
Raleigh	*Okay. Where is your home now?*
Jim	We … we are camped now by a river. In the foothills.
Raleigh	*Of what? Of what area? Of the Rocky Mountains?*
Jim	Yes. On … on … yes.
Raleigh	*Okay, did you ever marry in your life?*
Jim	No.
Raleigh	*Why?*
Jim	I … I died.
Raleigh	*Okay, what from?*
Jim	A bear. A grizzly bear.
Raleigh	*A grizzly bear? Okay ….*
Jim	It's a giant.
Raleigh	*Are there any of your tribe left alive today? No, I mean of your ancestors? Coming toward the present day.*
Jim	I see none.
Raleigh	*There are none? What happened to all of your people?*
Jim	We … we stayed … as one. We died as one.

Raleigh   *What did they die of? Did they die all at once or gradually?*

Jim   Bad winter. No food ....

Raleigh   *Was this ... was this in the past? Or had you already died?*

Jim   No, I was still alive.

Raleigh   *Okay, how many were left alive when you died?*

Jim   Twenty-four braves, good warriors.

Raleigh   *The strongest?*

Jim   Yes.

Raleigh   *Why didn't you try and get out of there?*

Jim   This is the way ... our ancestors lived. We must carry on, be proud.

Raleigh   *Even if it meant your death?*

Jim   If that is the way it should be.

Raleigh   *Did you fear death?*

Jim   No.

Raleigh   *Why?*

Jim   Proud to die with honor.

Raleigh   *Did you ever see a girl that you liked?*

Jim   It's forbidden.

Raleigh   *It was forbidden? You couldn't even look at one?*

Jim   Not with lust.

Raleigh   *Okay, but did you have any girls that were just your friends?*

Jim   No.

Raleigh   *No? You were ... did the braves stay together?*

Jim   Yes.

Raleigh   *Okay, how old did you have to be before you could marry?*

Jim   Twenty-two summers.

Raleigh   *Twenty-two. Okay. How old did the girl have to be?*

Jim	Sixteen summers.
Raleigh	*Okay.*
Jim	With ....
Raleigh	*With what?*
Jim	With your father having a … many, many good ponies; maybe 14, 15 summers.
Raleigh	*Okay. Did the braves ever get to marry early?*
Jim	It was forbidden.
Raleigh	*Okay, even if you could have bought your way, it was forbidden?*
Jim	A brave does not. Her father gives.
Raleigh	*I see, okay, I understand. What was the branch of your tribe? What other tribe did you come from?*
Jim	The Wichita.
Raleigh	*The Wichita Indians?*
Jim	Yes.
Raleigh	*Where are they from? Why are they called the Wichita Indians?*
Jim	They are Plains.
Raleigh	*They are Plains Indians, too?*
Jim	They … they are proud and peaceful people.
Raleigh	*Okay.*
Jim	They live … in sacred place.
Raleigh	*Where is the sacred place?*
Jim	Between two rivers.
Raleigh	*What were the rivers?*
Jim	I know not their names. My father has spoke to me about them.
Raleigh	*What did he tell you about them?*
Jim	They were peaceful people. The rivers protected them. And they, in turn, protected the rivers.

Raleigh	*Okay. Did you have friends other than Indians? Did you have white men that were friends?*
Jim	No.
Raleigh	*Did you ever see any white men?*
Jim	With the white girl. She ... she speaks without ... not with heart ....
Raleigh	*Okay, let me ask you ....*
Jim	... Kills ....
Raleigh	*Have you ever seen white men?*
Jim	Yes.
Raleigh	*Where?*
Jim	They have come to our camp.
Raleigh	*Okay, have they killed any of you?*
Jim	They killed my father's brother.
Raleigh	*Why?*
Jim.	Ponies.
Raleigh	*They stole his ponies?*
Jim	Yes.
Raleigh	*Alright, let's go up to the time you died. To the bear. We'll go gradually. Let's come back to the bear. Were you out by yourself that day? Remember, this has all happened, so just describe what happened.*
Jim	We ... we had take chase ... the hunting.
Raleigh	*Yes?*
Jim	It's a good day. The sun is hot.
Raleigh	*What were you hunting with?*
Jim	Bow.
Raleigh	*Okay.*
Jim	We ... gave chase. He goes ... goes down into the grove. I go into the sun, to come with the wind. Antelope ... take chase ... screams ... blood .... It's a giant one.

Raleigh	*Just describe. Remember, this has happened.*
Jim	He's … he's tearing them apart.
Raleigh	*Okay, just relax. This has all happened. It cannot be changed. You realize that, don't you?*
Jim	Yes.
Raleigh	*Okay, there's nothing you can do about it. Did he catch them from behind or where?*
Jim	Yes ….
Raleigh	*Relax.*
Jim	The brave ones, banding … picked them up … squealing.
Raleigh	*Okay, did you try to kill the bear?*
Jim	He's … he's four heads taller than ….
Raleigh	*Four heads taller? How tall would that be?*
Jim	Seven … seven-and-a-half feet maybe.
Raleigh	*Okay, and this is a grizzly bear?*
Jim	He's called it now.
Raleigh	*Okay, what did you call them?*
Jim	We called them many names.
Raleigh	*What were some of the names.*
Jim	Black Devil.
Raleigh	*No, in Indian, what were some of the names?*
Jim	Wha-Hawk-Naw.
Raleigh	*Was that Black Devil?*
Jim	Killer One Stalks.
Raleigh	*Okay. What are some Indian words that you can think of? What do they mean? How do you say hello? [Hand motion.] Just with your hand?*
Jim	Yes.
Raleigh	*What are some other hand signals that you know?*
Jim	I …. [Motion.]
Raleigh	*What does that mean?*

Jim   I come … in peace.

Raleigh   *Okay.*

Jim   In … peace ….

Raleigh   *What are some others? How do you say goodbye?*

Jim   There is no word.

Raleigh   *There is no word? Why?*

Jim   Your spirit … always remains.

Raleigh   *So you never say goodbye.*

Jim   No, if you come in good spirits, your spirit will always remain. You come in bad spirits, it makes your heart heavy.

Raleigh   *Okay. Do you speak more in hand signals or by mouth?*

Jim   By mouth.

Raleigh   *Okay, what do you say when you leave someone … for a period of time?*

Jim   You never leave. Your spirit is always there.

Raleigh   *Okay, but like when you go hunting. How do you tell someone, "I am going hunting"?*

Jim   Wa tee naw haw.

Raleigh   *Is that, "I'm going hunting"?*

Jim   I am going.

Raleigh   *Okay, good. Okay, are there any stories that you know about your ancestors? That are good … that are passed down and are really outstanding stories?*

Jim   Only the Council and braves can be … be honored to sit in the lodge. We ….

Raleigh   *Aren't you a brave?*

Jim   Yes.

Raleigh   *But you never heard any of the stories?*

Jim   Yes, but I cannot speak.

Raleigh   *Oh, okay! Okay, you cannot speak the stories.*

Jim   You must sit in the lodge.

Raleigh	*Oh, you have to be in the lodge to hear the stories?*
Jim	Yes.
Raleigh	*Why is that?*
Jim	To keep … to keep our past true.
Raleigh	*Okay. Did you ever ….*
Jim	Old women gossiped.
Raleigh	*Okay, alright, even in your tribe they gossip?*
Jim	Oh, yes. Gossip and complain.
Raleigh	*About what?*
Jim	Not enough food …. We don't want these ….
Raleigh	*We don't want what?*
Jim	This type of food.
Raleigh	*And what type of food don't they like?*
Jim	They … they don't … they don't … they don't like snake.
Raleigh	*Snake? Do you like snake?*
Jim	It's good.
Raleigh	*What's your favorite snake … are there different flavors of snake? I mean, does one snake taste different than another snake?*
Jim	All … all snakes taste the same.
Raleigh	*They do? What's your favorite food? And what don't you like … the worst?*
Jim	Squirrel.
Raleigh	*You like squirrel the best?*
Jim	No!
Raleigh	*You hate squirrel?*
Jim	Too many bones.
Raleigh	*Too many bones, okay. And what's your favorite?*
Jim	Antelope.
Raleigh	*Antelope, okay. Did your tribe ever have any tribal songs? Did you ever sing any songs?*

Jim	Yes. In the lodge.
Raleigh	*Okay, I would like to go to the lodge and listen to you sing a song, if you would.*
Jim	That cannot be allowed.
Raleigh	*Cannot be allowed. Can we go to a day that you sang a song ... in the lodge?*
Jim	I cannot. It is not allowed.
Raleigh	*Okay, were there any songs that the children may sing outside, you know, that would be allowed?*
Jim	Only ... only braves and council may sing. The spirit listens ... braves ... not old fool women and children.
Raleigh	*Okay, alright.*
Jim	They know not what they speak.
Raleigh	*Alright, did you ever paint, like pictures or things like this?*
Jim	We paint ... our face and hands.
Raleigh	*Do you paint well?*
Jim	My father tells me I need practice. He paints well.
Raleigh	*He paints well.*
Jim	Yes. He paints many councilmen.
Raleigh	*Okay. If I gave you something to paint with, could you paint a picture for me?*
Jim	We paint not many pictures.
Raleigh	*What do you paint?*
Jim	Paint ourselves.
Raleigh	*Paint yourselves, okay. Do you ever paint pictures?*
Jim	No, it is ... they are not allowed.
Raleigh	*Who is allowed?*
Jim	Mot ... Motoonay.
Raleigh	*Who's that?*

Jim	He is our speaker, as you call medicine man … lots of people … proud man.
Raleigh	*What is your talent? What are you good at?*
Jim	I am a warrior!
Raleigh	*A warrior. Okay, against people?*
Jim	I am a brave!
Raleigh	*Against people?*
Jim	Only … when to protect.
Raleigh	*Only to protect.*
Jim	You will … bad … bad … to take life out of anger.
Raleigh	*Okay, have you ever killed someone?*
Jim	Yes.
Raleigh	*Who?*
Jim	The three white men that killed my uncle.
Raleigh	*Okay, did you hunt them down?*
Jim	We came upon them. Yes … we beat them.
Raleigh	*Okay. Let's come back now, back, back to ….*
Jim	Four hides.
Raleigh	*They stole four hides from him, too?*
Jim	Yes.
Raleigh	*Did you get all your property back?*
Jim	Yes.
Raleigh	*Okay. Is there any test you have to do to become a brave?*
Jim	Yes.
Raleigh	*What is it?*
Jim	You must go out … and feed your father's family for a moon.
Raleigh	*How long is a moon?*
Jim	One full cycle of the moon.
Raleigh	*Is that the whole test?*
Jim	You must … be able to go … 12 suns … without eating.

Raleigh	*And what else?*
Jim	You must fight the other braves.
Raleigh	*With what?*
Jim	Clubs.
Raleigh	*Okay.*
Jim	Wrap clubs with hide. Perhaps six, seven braves coming at you. You fight. Council watches and they accept. If you are rejected, you must leave the tribe.
Raleigh	*Do many leave?*
Jim	Few. We are proud.
Raleigh	*Okay. Where do the people go that get rejected?*
Jim	They … they go into the clouds in the mountains. They say the Great Spirit … the Great One … He takes them and cleanses them and returns us to them as newborns.
Raleigh	*Okay, alright. Now, I want you to come back to the time when the bear killed you. The bear has killed you. Alright, are you there?*
Jim	Uh ….
Raleigh	*Alright, remember this has all happened. Hasn't it? Relax. Relax. You are describing. You are not reliving; you are describing. The bear has killed you. What happened after the bear killed you?*
Jim	The bear ….
Raleigh	*Relax.*
Jim	The black devil … he died with me.
Raleigh	*You killed him?*
Jim	I took him.
Raleigh	*Okay.*
Jim	I lay … I ask the Great Spirit to take me to the top of the mountains.
Raleigh	*Are you dead?*

Jim	And to the clouds.
Raleigh	*Wait, are you dead?*
Jim	No.
Raleigh	*Okay.*
Jim	I must pray before I die.
Raleigh	*Okay.*
Jim	I must ....
Raleigh	*Did you get ... did you get your prayer done?*
Jim	I would lay one ... one full sun. I am weak. My life flows from me.
Raleigh	*Okay.*
Jim	I ... am proud. I have died with honor!
Raleigh	*Okay, you have died, haven't you?*
Jim	Yes.
Raleigh	*Okay. Did anyone find you?*
Jim	Two suns later, my father ... and two other braves ... they find us. They take us into the mountain. My spirit ....
Raleigh	*Did you go with them?*
Jim	My spirit goes with my ... with my body, my soul.
Raleigh	*Okay, I understand. Alright ....*
Jim	I see my father. He wails words with a song. He is sorry.
Raleigh	*What did your father sing?*
Jim	[He sings the death chant. It is so hauntingly beautiful that it still gives me goose bumps each time I hear it. I have been told this is an authentic chant.] He chants he is sorry ... he is sorry for my death.
Raleigh	*Okay, was that the whole song or does he repeat it?*
Jim	He repeats. My father ... he is sorry. I ... want to reach out, touch him. I touch him but he feels me not.

Raleigh	*Okay, does your soul have substance?*
Jim	I know ... I know myself. I know myself but I have no me.
Raleigh	*Okay, very well. Alright, how long did you stay ... within earth?*
Jim	I saw ... saw all of this land.
Raleigh	*The entire earth?*
Jim	No. I saw ... I see ... I see ... a man with flaming yellow hair, many white men.
Raleigh	*Who is this man?*
Jim	I know him not. He has flaming yellow hair like the grass in the prairie.
Raleigh	*Okay, gold hair. Alright, who is this man? Who does he come to be?*
Jim	General George Armstrong Custer. I see him only shortly. I watch him die.
Raleigh	*Oh, you have not gone to heaven yet?*
Jim	No, my spirit wanders.
Raleigh	*Why did you watch George Armstrong Custer die?*
Jim	I know not why. My spirit takes me. I have no control.
Raleigh	*Okay, what did the general have to say at that time?*
Jim	He is proud of his many victories. He carries many scalps on his belt.
Raleigh	*Okay, is he dead at that time?*
Jim	No. He sits on a beautiful pony. His pony's colored like the river ... like river sand.
Raleigh	*Okay.*
Jim	He ... he tells ... he tells his council he will ... he will surprise them. He will kill.
Raleigh	*Okay.*

Jim	He will catch many … many in their lodges asleep. He will kill.
Raleigh	*Alright, okay. Now, let's … let's come ahead. How long did you wander the land?*
Jim	I see … I see … a car. My spirit soars.
Raleigh	*A car?*
Jim	A man on a road.
Raleigh	*What's the year that you see?*
Jim	I know not the time. The car is black. I know it's car; he calls it the car. Not … not like the white man's cart. No ponies.
Raleigh	*Okay.*
Jim	He … he strikes at the front of it. He makes me laugh. He kicks it.
Raleigh	*Okay.*
Jim	It has no soul … it will not hear him.
Raleigh	*Okay. Who is this man?*
Jim	I know him not. I see him briefly.
Raleigh	*Okay.*
Jim	I go.
Raleigh	*Okay. When you leave earth, where do you go?*
Jim	I know not the place … it's peaceful. One Great Spirit is taking me …. I may now rest. I sense spirits. I sense the soul of many a brave warrior … and white man. There is much, much friendship.
Raleigh	*Are you happy?*
Jim	Yes. We speak not. I feel is all. I have feeling … so peaceful. I am happy.

EPISODE 13

◆ A Lake ◆

I MET LEROY at one of my many lectures. He had come to an earlier session and returned later that evening hoping to be put under. He is a tall, black-haired teenager who originally came to stop smoking. Whenever people come for this purpose, I always ask if they really want to stop. Sometimes they admit, while under hypnosis, that they don't want to quit at that time. In those situations, I do not proceed. In Leroy's case, he was having tough times with his girlfriend and thought smoking helped him relax. I left the suggestion that whenever he needed to relax, he would just think of this session instead of feeling the need to smoke.

Much to our amusement, Leroy's cell phone rang every few minutes until his friend finally took it out of Leroy's pocket and answered it. We had to cut this session short because his mother was calling to remind him of a prior commitment.

This story is one of great hardship and the rewards that follow. It just goes to show that we are constantly being watched and our lives are being noted.

Raleigh	*We're going back in time. It's another time and another place, before you were born. What do you see?*
Leroy	A lake.
Raleigh	*What about the lake?*
Leroy	It's got a big rock in the middle.
Raleigh	*Okay, what else do you see about the lake?*

Leroy	It's dark. The water's dark.
Raleigh	*The water's dark?*
Leroy	And it's dark outside.
Raleigh	*Okay, where are you at?*
Leroy	Sitting on a hill.
Raleigh	*Looking down at the lake?*
Leroy	Umm hmm. Wondering how I can get out to that rock.
Raleigh	*Okay. How old are you?*
Leroy	A teenager.
Raleigh	*Alright, is there anyone with you?*
Leroy	Uh-uh.
Raleigh	*No? Okay, how are you dressed?*
Leroy	Looks like I'm wearing a toga.
Raleigh	*Okay, like a robe?*
Leroy	Yeah!
Raleigh	*Alright, what do you look like?*
Leroy	I … got blonde hair!
Raleigh	*Blonde hair, okay. How tall are you?*
Leroy	I don't know; I'm sitting down.
Raleigh	*Okay.*
Leroy	I can't see my face!
Raleigh	*Alright, is the hair long or short?*
Leroy	Medium.
Raleigh	*Okay. And you're wanting to go out to this rock?*
Leroy	Uh-huh.
Raleigh	*Any special reason why?*
Leroy	Uh-uh.
Raleigh	*No? Okay. Where did you come from? Let's go to a little earlier in the day. What do you see?*
Leroy	A village.
Raleigh	*Okay. Do you have a family?*

Leroy	I just see myself walking all over the village.
Raleigh	*Walking around the village, okay.*
Leroy	In the market.
Raleigh	*Okay. Are you tall, short, fat, thin?*
Leroy	Tall and thin.
Raleigh	*Do you see anyone in the village that you know?*
Leroy	Uh-uh.
Raleigh	*No? Is this your village?*
Leroy	I think so.
Raleigh	*Okay, continue on. Where did you come from earlier then that? You're in the village. Let's go back a bit farther. Where did you come from?*
Leroy	I slept on top of somebody's house!
Raleigh	*You slept on top of somebody's house?*
Leroy	Yeah, ha-ha, that's weird!
Raleigh	*Okay. Where is your family?*
Leroy	I don't know.
Raleigh	*Let's go farther back in time. Not necessarily that day, but farther back in time. Let's go back when you were … like 10, alright? Do you see your family?*
Leroy	They died in the plague.
Raleigh	*They died in the plague, is that correct?*
Leroy	Some kind of a disease.
Raleigh	*Your mom and your dad?*
Leroy	And a sister.
Raleigh	*How old was your sister?*
Leroy	Seven.
Raleigh	*What was her name?*
Leroy	Katrina.
Raleigh	*What was your mom's name?*
Leroy	I don't know.
Raleigh	*You didn't hear your mom's name?*

Leroy	No.
Raleigh	*What was your dad's name?*
Leroy	Daniel.
Raleigh	*What did your dad call your mom?*
Leroy	It starts with an "M".
Raleigh	*Just say it as he says it.*
Leroy	"Mabel."
Raleigh	*Mabel? Is that right?*
Leroy	Mabel.
Raleigh	*Okay, and what did they call you?*
Leroy	Timothy.
Raleigh	*And did you have a last name?*
Leroy	Uh-uh.
Raleigh	*No, just Timothy?*
Leroy	Yeah.
Raleigh	*Okay, that's all you ever heard?*
Leroy	Uh-huh.
Raleigh	*Alright. What country are you from?*
Leroy	I don't know.
Raleigh	*Alright. Do you live in town or in the country at 10?*
Leroy	In town.
Raleigh	*Let's go now to that town. What is the name of your town?*
Leroy	Lin … something.
Raleigh	*Okay, say it as they say it.*
Leroy	"Lindesborough."
Raleigh	*Is that what they call it?*
Leroy	Yeah.
Raleigh	*Who said that?*
Leroy	A farmer.
Raleigh	*A farmer, is that right?*
Leroy	Yeah.

Raleigh	*At 10, is your family already gone?*
Leroy	My mom died.
Raleigh	*Your mom died?*
Leroy	Yeah.
Raleigh	*What were the characteristics of the plague?*
Leroy	They turned green.
Raleigh	*The people turned green?*
Leroy	Yeah … they got fuzzy.
Raleigh	*Their skin got fuzzy?*
Leroy	Yeah … looked like olives on them.
Raleigh	*And it looked like olives on them? Like blisters?*
Leroy	Yeah.
Raleigh	*Did this plague take a long time to kill someone?*
Leroy	About a month.
Raleigh	*Okay. How did your mom come down with it?*
Leroy	She went into town, to market; about a week later, she was coughing.
Raleigh	*Were there a lot of people dying from this?*
Leroy	Not in my neighborhood … it was inside the city wall.
Raleigh	*So you lived outside the city wall?*
Leroy	Yeah.
Raleigh	*Somewhere in the course of time, someone gave the year. What is the year?*
Leroy	1713.
Raleigh	*1713. Okay, who got the plague next?*
Leroy	They both died.
Raleigh	*Your father and your sister?*
Leroy	Yeah.
Raleigh	*How was it transmitted? How did they catch it?*
Leroy	I don't know.
Raleigh	*What did you do?*

Leroy	I brought them water.
Raleigh	*Your brought them water, okay. Did you catch it at all?*
Leroy	Not at all.
Raleigh	*Was there a doctor?*
Leroy	He was stupid.
Raleigh	*He was stupid?*
Leroy	He was stupid! He only came once.
Raleigh	*What was his idea of a cure?*
Leroy	Laying down by the fire.
Raleigh	*So he wanted them to sweat it out?*
Leroy	Just lay down by the fire.
Raleigh	*Did you actually bring your family water or just stick it inside the door?*
Leroy	It was just a big living room with a fireplace.
Raleigh	*So you brought water in to them?*
Leroy	Yes, it was like a bucket.
Raleigh	*What did your father do for a living?*
Leroy	He was a blacksmith.
Raleigh	*So he was a fairly strong man?*
Leroy	Yes, and hairy, too.
Raleigh	*Ha-ha, and hairy?*
Leroy	Yes.
Raleigh	*How is he dressed when you see him?*
Leroy	It looks like he's wearing like some type of pants and a white shirt.
Raleigh	*What country are you in?*
Leroy	Europe, I don't know.
Raleigh	*Are you in mountains, plains, what?*
Leroy	Hilly.
Raleigh	*Do you see mountains?*
Leroy	Too many buildings, houses.

Raleigh	*Does it get cold there?*
Leroy	Winter time.
Raleigh	*What time of year is it right now?*
Leroy	Spring.
Raleigh	*And this is when your dad and sister got sick. How long did it take for them to die?*
Leroy	My dad died first, then about a week later my sister.
Raleigh	*Did you try to feed them?*
Leroy	All I had was tomatoes.
Raleigh	*Tomatoes? Did you have money?*
Leroy	No.
Raleigh	*So where did you get the tomatoes?*
Leroy	I sold stuff.
Raleigh	*Like what?*
Leroy	Left-over stuff that my dad had made.
Raleigh	*What were some of those items?*
Leroy	Handcuffs.
Raleigh	*He had handcuffs!*
Leroy	Yeah.
Raleigh	*Did he teach you how to do any of the blacksmith work?*
Leroy	Kind of.
Raleigh	*What were the handcuffs made for?*
Leroy	I don't know.
Raleigh	*But he sold them?*
Leroy	Yeah.
Raleigh	*Okay. You never got the disease?*
Leroy	No.
Raleigh	*Did a lot more people in the area get it?*
Leroy	Yeah, that's why I left.
Raleigh	*So that's why you left, at age 10?*
Leroy	About 12.

Raleigh *So it got bad, then what did you do to stay alive?*

Leroy I would help people. They would give me food, let me stay at their homes.

Raleigh *So you knew some of these people?*

Leroy Yeah.

Raleigh *What did you do with your parents' home?*

Leroy I left.

Raleigh *You didn't try to sell it?*

Leroy No.

Raleigh *Were you worried you might get the disease?*

Leroy No, I would have already had it.

Raleigh *Did you bury your family?*

Leroy Burned them.

Raleigh *You burned them?*

Leroy The mayor.

Raleigh *The mayor burned them? Did anyone help you burn them?*

Leroy There was a big pile.

Raleigh *Yes, but you are not very big. How did you do it?*

Leroy They came with a big wheelbarrow.

Raleigh *Did they burn your house?*

Leroy Uh-uh. They took it down and burned the roof in the pile.

Raleigh *Was this so nobody would live in it?*

Leroy I don't know.

Raleigh *Okay. At 12 you left, so where did you go?*

Leroy I had a donkey, or mule. I think I stole it.

Raleigh *You stole it? Okay, where did you go?*

Leroy I walked a long time. I ate a bunch of apples, crossed a lot of rivers.

Raleigh *So you went a long ways?*

Leroy Yeah.

Raleigh	*How old are you now, after you made this long trip?*
Leroy	Thirteen or fourteen. It was a long year.
Raleigh	*Why did you take a donkey if you didn't ride it?*
Leroy	I would pack it up with apples.
Raleigh	*Did you sell the apples or keep them for yourself?*
Leroy	I ate them; I was hungry.
Raleigh	*Did you live to see 20?*
Leroy	Twenty?
Raleigh	*Yes. [Long pause.] Had the disease gone to where you are?*
Leroy	I didn't see anything.
Raleigh	*Okay, how old did you live to be?*
Leroy	I don't know.
Raleigh	*What was the last age you remember?*
Leroy	Fifteen, walking around the market.
Raleigh	*Was this before or after you were sitting, looking at the rock?*
Leroy	The market is before.
Raleigh	*So you remember sitting on the hill, looking at the rock?*
Leroy	Yeah, and the dark water.
Raleigh	*So what did you end up doing?*
Leroy	I was up there thinking.
Raleigh	*Yeah?*
Leroy	How was I going to get to that rock? It was a long ways.
Raleigh	*Could you swim?*
Leroy	Not very good.
Raleigh	*What time of year is it?*
Leroy	Fall.
Raleigh	*So did you try to go to the rock?*
Leroy	That's all that I can remember.

Raleigh	*What happened that day? You don't have to feel it, just tell about it.*
Leroy	At the lake?
Raleigh	*Yes, what happened that day?*
Leroy	I think I fell asleep.
Raleigh	*You fell asleep?*
Leroy	Uh-huh.
Raleigh	*Did you wake up the next day?*
Leroy	No.
Raleigh	*So you are sitting up on the hill, looking at the rock. Did you die that night?*
Leroy	Sometime.
Raleigh	*What happened? Don't feel it. Just tell me.*
Leroy	I just was real tired … really tired.
Raleigh	*Were you hungry?*
Leroy	Not anymore.
Raleigh	*Were you hungry before you fell asleep?*
Leroy	Yeah.
Raleigh	*Very hungry? Had it been a long time since you've eaten?*
Leroy	Yeah.
Raleigh	*Days?*
Leroy	Umm hmm, somebody stole my donkey.
Raleigh	*So it had been days?*
Leroy	Yeah.
Raleigh	*So you sat down and you never woke up, correct?*
Leroy	Uh-huh.
Raleigh	*What happened after that? You're not hungry anymore.*
Leroy	Uh-uh.
Raleigh	*So you left your body?*
Leroy	I don't know.

Raleigh	*Alright, tell me what happens next. Where did you go from there?*
Leroy	I'm floating.
Raleigh	*Yes?*
Leroy	I'm floating into the clouds.
Raleigh	*Continue on.*
Leroy	I floated everywhere.
Raleigh	*Where did you go? What did you see? Did you see anything interesting?*
Leroy	I went over the ocean.
Raleigh	*Okay, what took you there?*
Leroy	The wind.
Raleigh	*Let's go to where you quit floating. Did you see your father or mother?*
Leroy	I don't know … I just floated for a long time.
Raleigh	*Okay, where did you go from there?*
Leroy	A big, white planet.
Raleigh	*Okay. Is it pretty?*
Leroy	Yeah! It looks like a big cloud inside.
Raleigh	*Okay, and who was there?*
Leroy	That was heaven!
Raleigh	*That was heaven. What were you told when you reached heaven?*
Leroy	I've done well. "My son, enjoy the fruit."
Raleigh	*You have, "Done well, My son, enjoy the fruit"?*
Leroy	"The fruits of your life are the fruits of your trials. Enjoy the fruits of your trials."
Raleigh	*The fruits of your life are the fruits of your trials?*
Leroy	"Enjoy the fruits of your trials."
Raleigh	*Enjoy the fruits of your trials. Did you see who actually said that?*
Leroy	The gate said it.

Raleigh	*At the gate?*
Leroy	Just the gate.
Raleigh	*What did the gate look like?*
Leroy	It was white, and it had gold things on top.
Raleigh	*And you heard this very clearly, then?*
Leroy	Uh-huh.
Raleigh	*So where did you go then?*
Leroy	And there is a big book.
Raleigh	*A big book?*
Leroy	Uh-huh, a big book.
Raleigh	*And what about the big book?*
Leroy	It had my name in it.
Raleigh	*Your name was in it? You were shown the book?*
Leroy	I just saw an old guy looking through it.
Raleigh	*Ha-ha, an old guy looking through it? And what did the old guy look like?*
Leroy	He had a big beard.
Raleigh	*A big beard?*
Leroy	A big, white beard … and he was bald.
Raleigh	*Alright. How is this man dressed?*
Leroy	Toga.
Raleigh	*A toga, what color?*
Leroy	White.
Raleigh	*Just white?*
Leroy	Pearl white … very, very bright white.
Raleigh	*Very bright white. Did this man look at you?*
Leroy	Yes, he was nice.
Raleigh	*He was nice, and what did he say?*
Leroy	He opened the gate!
Raleigh	*He opened the gate, and you went in?*
Leroy	Yes!

EPISODE 14

◆ Wheat Fields ◆

ONE NEVER KNOWS what surprises your travels will turn up. I thought this book was finished until I made a stop in Santa Nella, California, and met four very nice young ladies operating the check-in counter at my hotel. Once they discovered I was a hypnotist, we had a very interesting week when each young woman told an intriguing story while under hypnosis. I chose Deanna's story for the final episode after my wife and I talked about how unique it was. So — to Heather, Stephanie, Carrie, and Deanna — thank you for your trust, and I feel like we have made permanent friendships.

This book has been a travel through time and a testimony that life continues on even after our physical shells have long since deteriorated away. I want it to be a road map of hope showing that, if we live our lives to the best of our potentials, we will end up in heaven. Yet, how many of us are perfect? What happens to those who fall a little — or even quite a bit — short? There has to be a way to rectify our mistakes. Just because your children don't always do what they should, does that mean you turn your back and forget about them? I don't think so, and I'm sure God doesn't either. Now, that does not mean that everything is okay. There is always a reaction to an action. Each of the stories you have read has had its own personal solution. We are all individuals and viewed as such. We are given every opportunity to get life right. Naturally, the best time would be while we are living, but circumstances do happen.

With that in mind, we will now meet Deanna. As a young, single mother of two, she works very hard as a receptionist at a hotel. She has a bright personality and is pleasant to be around. After our session, Deanna understood why she hates fish and loves to be surrounded by people.

Although the following story is quite short, it packs a profound message. We did not have a recording device along for the word-by-word transcript, but our notes were quite good.

Raleigh	*We are now going to another time, another place before you were born. A place you know nothing of. What do you see?*
Deanna	A tree.
Raleigh	*A tree. Okay, is it a big tree, a small tree? What?*
Deanna	It's a big tree. It has a large round top.
Raleigh	*Where are you in relation to the tree?*
Deanna	I am in a field.
Raleigh	*Is there anyone with you?*
Deanna	No, I am alone.
Raleigh	*What type of a field is it?*
Deanna	It's a wheat field.
Raleigh	*What time of the year is it? Better yet, what does the wheat look like at this moment?*
Deanna	It's all gold.
Raleigh	*Okay, where are you in relation to this field?*
Deanna	I'm laying down in it.
Raleigh	*Look at yourself. What are you wearing?*
Deanna	It appears to be a white dress, long.
Raleigh	*What do you look like?*
Deanna	I have long, gold, curly hair.
Raleigh	*Are you pretty?*
Deanna	Yes, I would say so.

Raleigh	How old are you?
Deanna	Twenty-three.
Raleigh	What type of day is it?
Deanna	It's warm and breezy.
Raleigh	Where do you live?
Deanna	I don't know.
Raleigh	Okay. Let's go a little earlier, before you were in the field. What do you see?
Deanna	I'm by a creek. My dress is a peasant dress.
Raleigh	Okay. You are by a creek, but where do you live?
Deanna	In the mountains. It's a rock home.
Raleigh	What do you mean? Like a cave?
Deanna	No, it's a house made out of stone.
Raleigh	Do you have a family?
Deanna	No, I live alone.
Raleigh	Now, what is your name?
Deanna	I don't know.
Raleigh	At one time you had a family. Let's go to a time where you heard your name. What do you see?
Deanna	My dad.
Raleigh	Okay, how old are you?
Deanna	I'm six years old.
Raleigh	What was your father calling you?
Deanna	Leilah.
Raleigh	When you heard this name, what was taking place?
Deanna	I was being called to supper.
Raleigh	What year is this?
Deanna	I don't know.
Raleigh	Just allow it to come. What year is it?
Deanna	1839.
Raleigh	Okay. Where do you live?
Deanna	Norway.

Raleigh	Okay, now what do people call your father?
Deanna	Jim.
Raleigh	Jim, is that right?
Deanna	Yes.
Raleigh	Okay, Jim what? Does he have a last name?
Deanna	Phillips.
Raleigh	Alright, Jim Phillips. How does your father make a living?
Deanna	He cuts wood.
Raleigh	Okay. You said you lived alone, what happened?
Deanna	My father died.
Raleigh	What did he die from?
Deanna	I don't know. He just got sick.
Raleigh	Were there other people around?
Deanna	No, we didn't live near town.
Raleigh	Did you ever go to a town?
Deanna	Yes, once.
Raleigh	How old were you then?
Deanna	Fifteen.
Raleigh	Why did you go?
Deanna	My father was ill. I went to get fruit.
Raleigh	What did you think of the town?
Deanna	It was scary.
Raleigh	What did you normally eat?
Deanna	Fish.
Raleigh	Okay, did you have money?
Deanna	No.
Raleigh	So how did you plan to purchase the fruit?
Deanna	I took wood.
Raleigh	So did anyone buy the wood?
Deanna	No.
Raleigh	Did the people know your father was ill?

Deanna No, I didn't tell them.

Raleigh *Did you have any other family?*

Deanna No.

Raleigh *What about your mother? What happened to her?*

Deanna She died a long time ago, before I can remember.

Raleigh *Okay. Let's come up in time. Did you see age 25?*

Deanna Yes.

Raleigh *Okay, what are you doing?*

Deanna Fishing.

Raleigh *Okay. Do you have a family?*

Deanna No, I never married.

Raleigh *How are you at age 25?*

Deanna I have poor health, and I am very weak.

Raleigh *What are you wearing?*

Deanna A kind of blue and white dress.

Raleigh *Okay, so where did you get the clothes?*

Deanna I made them.

Raleigh *Okay, so where did you get the cloth to make the clothes?*

Deanna I got it from the bed linens.

Raleigh *Well, I have to hand it to you, I wouldn't have thought of that. Let's go on. Did you see age 30?*

Deanna No.

Raleigh *Did you see age 29?*

Deanna No.

Raleigh *Did you see age 28?*

Deanna No.

Raleigh *Did you see age 27?*

Deanna Some of it.

Raleigh *Okay, what are you doing?*

Deanna I am sad, alone, and sitting at the creek.

Raleigh *Is this the day you die?*

Deanna   Yes.

Raleigh   *I don't want you to feel what happened but to just tell me about it. Do you understand? You are just describing. Okay?*

Deanna   Yes.

Raleigh   *What happened to you?*

Deanna   I had a sick stomach.

Raleigh   *How long had you been sick?*

Deanna   Eighteen months.

Raleigh   *Once again, what happened?*

Deanna   I had been sick a long time. I am sad and alone. It was too much for me. I plunged into the water and took my own life.

Raleigh   *Did anyone ever find you?*

Deanna   No.

Raleigh   *What happened next? Where did you go from there?*

Deanna   It's like the wheat fields again. I am in the center of them. It is so peaceful.

Raleigh   *Okay, but let's travel on. Where did you go next?*

Deanna   [Large smile.] It's so bright! There is a gate with gold pillars.

Raleigh   *Do you see anyone?*

Deanna   Yes. It is so pretty. I see a man. He has a book.

Raleigh   *What does this man look like?*

Deanna   He is all dressed in a white flowing robe. It looks almost transparent and is moving as though in a breeze. He has brownish-colored hair and a brown beard.

Raleigh   *What is he telling you?*

Deanna   He is looking, but he is telling me he cannot find my name in the book.

Raleigh   *So you can see the book?*

Deanna	Yes, but I am not in it.
Raleigh	*What did he tell you?*
Deanna	"You must return to try again. Go back, live again; find Jesus so you may enter upon these pages."
Raleigh	*So have you helped Deanna?*
Deanna	Yes.
Raleigh	*What have you done for her?*
Deanna	I helped to show her the way.
Raleigh	*In what way did you do this?*
Deanna	To put her in the direction of people who care about her and brought her back to church.

When Deanna woke up, she was amazed but not upset. She was able to recount what she had just seen. I asked if she could still remember the book, and she said, "Very much so, yes."

Deanna said the book was the "Book of Life" and Leilah's name wasn't there; yet she knew being on the pages was not impossible. When she was asked how long it would take, she quickly answered, "Judgment Day."

CONCLUSION

◆ My Final Thoughts ◆

I SINCERELY HOPE you found these episodes as enjoyable to experience as it was for me to share them with you. Even 30-plus years later, I am just as intrigued by the stories that appear today as I was that very first time. As I wrote earlier, I wanted to include stories that covered not only a large span of time, but also a variety of interests.

I feel very fortunate that my life was enlightened that day so many years ago in Kansas City. The road has not always been smooth. Even after all these years, I still meet those hard-nosed individuals who think they are always correct and refuse to view life from any other perspective. In 1984 I lost my five-year-old son in an accident in front of our home. This was no doubt the lowest event of my life. It was during this time that I began using my method of regressed-life hypnosis to search for missing children. The system works, and I have never charged for my services. Even though I was helping families find their missing children, I was highly criticized by the church my family attended. My children became the victims of religious intolerance. If we could only open our minds, there are amazing things to be discovered every day.

As time passes on, I find that it is not an accident the way our lives cross paths, but that it is up to the individual which direction to take. Many times when I give lectures or demonstrations, people tell me they changed their plans so they could watch or participate in what I do instead. While these people were under, most said God told them that we would meet. What I find interesting is that I have done this all over the world with the same results. No matter who or where we are, there is a bond between all of us on the other side.

By reading the previous episodes, you have made up your mind that this is either total nonsense or possibly one of the best discoveries you have ever heard. I hope you pick the second choice, but it is still your own view.

It is difficult to explain my observations of past lives. Each past life varies slightly from one to the next because there is a certain amount of individuality. I never know who I will find during a first session. You have read only a few transcripts, but I have lost count of how many people I have regressed over the years.

Each past life is here for a specific purpose. Sometimes the individual needs to learn how to become humble. Sometimes they are here to experience childbirth and raising a family. Others are here just to help us get through the rough spots in our lives. The list goes on and on, but I think you get the idea. In the process, the past life grows through your experiences. The manner in which you conduct your life has a direct impact on the past life.

I have found that if the helper led a pretty good life when alive, then he or she will have some options after death. One option is choosing who to come back to assist. For example, if the helper never had children of her own, she has the opportunity to come back and experience childbirth, raising a family, and all of the joys and sorrows that go along with it. They are shown different life lines — as I like to call them — and then make their choice. These pre-birth selections show that there are certain aspects of our lives already mapped out for us. I believe we have a basic road to follow and that it ends in a certain destination: death. Now, there are many small roads — life's obstacles — off the main highway to choose from. The more correct way to the destination is not always the easiest to follow; but according to statements given by countless past lives, it pays off when it is your turn to enter the other side.

The flip side of the coin is that if the helper did not live as good a life when alive as he should have, then he has to work harder. These helpers must learn from past mistakes and try to help us avoid similar pitfalls in our present lives. They are very limited in what they can do and, for the most part, can act only as your conscience by giving you the feeling of right and wrong. In both instances, the helper is trying to purify himself while helping you get to a better position after you die.

I have been asked how many past lives we can have. I know people have claimed to have had several past lives; but in all the years that I have been doing regressions, I have found that each of us is only assigned one. Over the years that one past life may have been back a few times to help other people, so maybe that is where the confusion comes from.

Another question people have is if a past life can be of a different gender than that of the person I am working with. This has never occurred in any of the regressions I have done. As you have read, helpers can be of a different race. Just as society claims: it has nothing to do with the color of your skin but what's inside — your spirit — that counts.

If you wonder what past life is assisting you, just examine who you are. A certain amount of their life is intertwined with yours. You may have strong feelings about a specific time in history. You may do things that others think are odd but feel quite everyday and normal to you. Remember, this is like a partnership, so what is good for one is shared by the other.

I think that life on the other side is fair and just. I believe the love of one's family is not lost after death and that we will see our loved ones again. I never felt that if a person did wrong while alive, then hell was their final destination without other options. From what I have seen, God is very forgiving and does everything to help us cleanse our spirits. I do not know what happens to people like Hitler, serial killers, or those into the black arts and devil worship. I am not the one judging their souls, so I will not even venture a guess.

I know that suicide is forgiven because I have run across that scenario. The individual is given few abilities and begins the process from almost a fresh start. Once again, though, they were greeted by a huge amount of love and tenderness. I am very pleased by these findings, since the question is brought up far too many times by the survivors of individuals who have taken their own lives.

Our lives are filled with questions like why did this have to happen to those people or why did this have to happen to my family? Once again, some of these events are pre-set and cannot be changed. In the event of the death of my son, he told me from the other side that he selected my family to be born into. He knew he would only live a short life, but he could assist me better from the other side.

I know these concepts are hard to understand, and sometimes the answers I get really make me stop and think for a while. I can tell you that I have witnessed things beyond ordinary explanation. I have drawings that past lives sketched of abductors in missing children cases that are so accurate it is as though the individuals posed for them.

Once, I used a past life to help diagnose the location of a seed tumor in a friend's brain. He had already had brain surgery to remove the cancer, but it returned immediately. My friend was told he only had a very short time to live, but I felt he had a lot of life left in him. I used a past life to see if he was to die at that time and the answer was, "No." When I asked what could be done, the response came quickly. The past life sketched a picture of my friend's head — minus one ear because he was deaf in that ear. I did not know if that was accurate, but my friend later told me this was very true and that was why he always turned his head slightly when we talked. A tumor was drawn in the lower part of the back of the head, with lines indicating veins to the growth. The past life said a procedure of laser surgery [which did not exist several years ago when this was occurring] would cut off the blood supply to the growth and kill the tumor, but the rest of the growth would return to normal tissue. We were told this growth was missed by the X-rays, and he needed to be tested again.

My friend went back to his doctor and insisted he be checked again even though his doctor thought all the tumors had already been found. Wrong! The tumor was right where it had been drawn.

The next problem was what to do about it. Remember, the suggested procedure did not exist at that time. It has only been in the last few years science has discovered that cutting off the blood supply to certain cancers will stop them from growing and spreading. However, there was an experimental drug that was supposed to cut off the blood supply to cancerous tissue. After taking this drug, all the cancer in his brain went away. He later told me his doctor said whoever gave him that information must have an extensive knowledge of medicine in order to have found the cancer the first X-rays missed.

The individual I chose for this experiment was a maintenance electrician from a local aircraft plant. It was his past life who did the necessary work. Amazingly, the entire session took less than 15 minutes from start to finish.

Sadly, my friend has passed away from a non-related cause. He was able to live eight more years even though he had once been told he only had weeks left. He has been sorely missed.

I find the information given in these sessions is always accurate, but at times it is like those old science books with plastic lay-overs of the human body. First it shows you the entire human body. Turn the page and you see the muscles. Turn the next page to see the internal organs. Then, finally, the next page is the skeleton. The same is true when researching a specific location or time frame of events. When working on a missing-person case, the past life may be describing a specific location as it looked during their lifetime instead of today. Over the years I have been able to clear up most of these problems. Some people may mistakenly think they have more than one past life when it is really a blending of the plastic pages in the lay-over.

Earlier in this book a small note was mentioned about the first session I did more than 30 years ago. I asked that past life if my girlfriend and I would be together in the future, and the answer was, "No." As predicted, I moved away shortly thereafter, and we went our separate ways. Since that time, there have been a few instances when I have asked for advance views into someone's life. The last time I did this was several years ago at a New Year's Eve party. During the session, I was talking to the young boy from medieval England who was later killed alongside his father by some less-than-kind knights. I asked this boy about the future of his host, who was asleep in front of me. The future was simple: he was going to live in a home on wheels and there would be another child in the family. When I woke the individual, there were a lot of laughs about this prediction. There were especially a lot of laughs about there being another child in the family because he'd had a vasectomy. Well, the future is not always kind. As predicted, he purchased a mobile home, and his wife had another baby. Need I say more? It is because of that session, however, that I no longer go into the future of an individual unless it is for the purpose of helping someone, as was the case with my friend who had cancer.

A few years ago my wife and I took a trip to Egypt, and one wish I had was to hypnotize one of the local people. Our trip included a seven-day cruise down the Nile, with a stop at the Temple of Dendera. The ship was going to spend the night after a fabulous tour of the ancient complex. I sensed an energy in the Temple and wanted to return that evening, but because there was trouble in the area no one was allowed off the ship. Although the trouble was between the locals and had nothing to do with Americans, the cruise line did not want anyone to get hurt.

We were left with an open evening to get to know each other. When our tour's Egyptologist asked why I wanted to go back to the Temple that evening, I told her what I had sensed. She said the caretakers of the complex talk about the "old ones" who walk the halls at night. She felt that was just foolish and surely I could not believe in such things. I could not have had a better opportunity to discuss these subjects and my love of hypnosis. That night I did three sessions with Egyptians who knew nothing of my work in regression. As usual, each had a past life who told about living in a previous time and about life after death.

Once again, some things are meant to happen. One man said he was supposed to be on vacation but was called back to work when a fellow crew member broke his leg (which occurred at the same time as our flight to Egypt). He told me he was angry at first, but after what he just saw he was glad that he was called back. Our paths were meant to cross.

Several years ago a group of friends and I started looking

into the future of mankind as a whole. At first, the information was pretty limited. As time passed, we were allowed to see more, including the war that is now occurring. When I hypnotized the cruise director that evening in Egypt, I took him five years into the future of mankind. Once again, we saw war. Even though we were not given a reason for the war, we were told that it would get much worse before it gets better.

We have been told that there is still a chance to clean up our acts and become better individuals toward one another. We have also been told that we have not learned all we need to know at the present time and we have progressed very little. When you stop to think about it, this statement is very true. We may have supersonic airplanes, televisions, microwave ovens, and air conditioning for our comfort, but we also have more ways to kill, hate, and destroy than ever thought possible. We are the ones responsible for our lives, as well as our treatment of others. Our helpers are here to assist us to that next level where everyone is the same. When will that day come? I do not really know. I have not asked, and I am not sure I would be given the answer if I did. I do know I would like to be around when it happens.

Thank you for allowing me to share a part of my life with you. I hope it gives you a little insight into the other side. I also hope it answers some of your questions about what happens to loved ones when they pass on. No matter what religion they are, people from around the world have seen that there is life on the other side and that we are all joined at the soul. The episodes you have just read illustrate that your loved ones are always close by. Remember, just because they are no longer in their physical forms does not mean they are gone from your side. Talk to them because they will hear you.

This was drawn by a past life during regression. It shows how people appear on the other side.